WORLD'S FAIR NOTES

A Woman Journalist Views Chicago's

1893 Columbian Exposition

by Marian Shaw

COVER DRAWINGS ADOPTED FROM:

*A Brief History of the Invention and Construction of The Ferris Wheel, Together with
a Short Bibliography of George W. G. Ferris, Esq.*
Chicago: The Ferris Wheel Co., 1893.

ILLUSTRATION CREDITS:

J. B. Campbell. *Campbell's Illustrated History of the
World's Columbian Exposition.* Philadelphia: Sessler &
Dongan, 1894 [For the illustrations at pages 31, 33, 42, and 54.]

Handbook to the World's Columbian Exposition.
Chicago: Rand, McNally & Company, Publishers, 1893
[For the illustrations at pages 18 and 62.]

The Dream City. St. Louis: N. D. Thompson Publishers, 1893
[For the illustrations at pages 20, 24, 27, 37, 48, 58, and 73.]

Trumbull White and William Igleheart. *The World's Columbian
Exposition, Chicago, 1893.* Philadelphia: World Publishing Co., 1893.
[For the illustration at page 89.]

Special Collections Department, Northwestern University Library,
Evanston, Illinois [For the photograph of Teresa Dean at page 84.]

Archives, General Federation of Women's Clubs,
Washington, D. C.
[For the photograph of Jennie June Croly at page 85.]

Frances Benjamin Johnston Papers. Archives, Library of Congress,
Washington, D. C. [For the photograph "Illumination at Night" at page 87 and for
the photograph of Susan B. Anthony at page 95.]

Lilian Whiting, *Kate Field, a Record.* Boston: Little, Brown and Company, 1889.
[For the photograph of Kate Field at page 92.]

Ida B. Wells Papers, The University of Chicago Library.
[For the photograph of Ida B. Wells at page 98.]

In Remembrance of the World's Columbian Exposition, Chicago.
New York: American Souvenir and Advertising Company, 1893.
[For the illustrations at pages 6 and 7.]

Maurice Minton, Ed. *Illustrated American Magazine. World's Fair Special Number.*
September, 1893. [For the illustrations at pages 39, 46, and 63.]

DEDICATION

We dedicate this book to Bonnie Harris, a native of Chicago, who made many visits to the World's Columbian Exposition and collected for us various souvenirs and documents. We also dedicate this book to her daughter, Eleanor Harris, who discovered the Marian Shaw articles and whose continuing and vital interest in the subject caused us to proceed with its publication.

CONTENTS

INTRODUCTION

A TALENTED AUTHOR AND JOURNALIST, now forgotten, wrote this series of articles for an obscure newspaper. She described with great precision, insight, and skill, her visits to the 1893 World's Columbian Exposition. That World's Fair was a conspicuous showcase of all aspects of then human endeavor, whether they were objects of culture, beauty, or utility. 27,529,400 people attended the Fair between May 1, 1893 and October 30, 1893.

The site of the Fair was in Jackson Park on the south side of Chicago, adjacent to Lake Michigan. The area was four times as large as that for any previous international exposition. There were a number of principal buildings, including those housing exhibits relating to manufacturing, machinery, agriculture, electricity, mines, transportation and fisheries, as well as buildings devoted to the arts, forestry, anthropology and dairy, and finally, one of

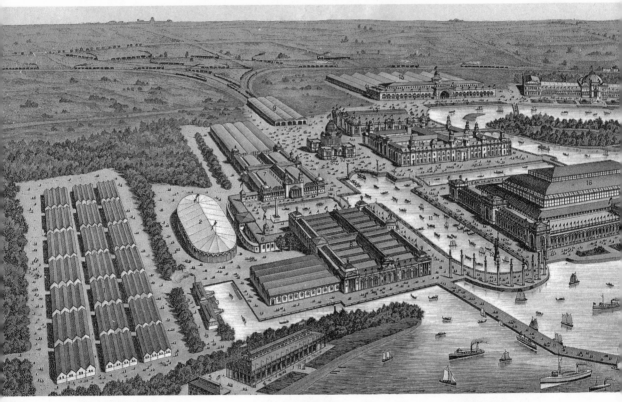

Bird's eye view of the World's Columbian Exposition, Chicago, 1893.

1. EXPOSITION OF BEASTS
2. ASSEMBLY HALL
3. SAW MILLS
4. FORESTRY
5. DAIRY
6. CONGRESS ROOMS
7. MACHINERY HALL
8. AGRICULTURAL BUILDING
9. RAILWAY STATION
10. ADMINISTRATION BUILDING
11. LAGOON
12. STATUE OF LIBERTY

particular interest to the author, the Woman's building. In addition to the Midway Plaisance and its innovative Ferris Wheel, eighty-six foreign countries and colonies had exhibits, and sixteen had their own buildings. Thirty-eight different states of the United States had their own buildings as well.

One of the historians who helped to document the Chicago Fair was Hubert Howe Bancroft. The preface to his 1893 work, *The Book of the Fair*, contained the following statement:

> Of the several world's fairs which have been held, little now remains in the way of description save what has been preserved in books. In due time, their purpose accomplished, most of the buildings of the present Exposition, these splendid edifices which have been reared to science, art, and industry, and to which all the world has made its pilgrimage, will be taken apart, and their contents removed. All that will be left of this brilliant spectacle will be in the minds of men and in printer's ink.

We hope that Marian Shaw's articles, now presented here and made available to the reading public, will be of some small illumination of an important event which occurred nearly a century ago.

13. MINES AND MINING BUILDING	18. HORTICULTURAL HALL	24. ILLINOIS STATE BUILDING
14. ELECTRICAL BUILDING	19. FOREIGN VILLAGES	25. PALACE OF FINE ARTS
15. TRANSPORTATION BUILDING	20. WOMAN'S BUILDING	26. BATTLE SHIP
16. MANUFACTURERS AND LIBERAL ARTS BUILDING	21. CASINO AND PIER	27. CHICAGO
17. PARK ISLAND	22. THE FEDERAL BUILDING	
	23. FISHERIES AND AQUARIUM BUILDING	

PREFACE

M Y OWN LIFE as a Chicago-born foreign correspondent has been one of classic adventure, of constant risk, of strange and unexpected meetings, of chance and jeopardy, and of St. Exupery's "accidents of journeying." When I think back over the years, I think of "adventure" in terms of blood red sunsets over the Red Sea and the falcons of Saudi princes sitting tethered in the plane seats just behind me; I think of flying over Tierra del Fuego in a tiny and fragile plane to find a wanted Nazi in a remote fishing village; and I remember a bitter battlefield on the Iraqi desert, with Iranian soldiers, frozen in death, scattered about like grotesquely disfigured rocks.

Those kinds of memories, the average person would agree, are what we normally think of as "adventures." The true adventurer is one who is Casablanca-ing it through the world, constantly murmuring dramatically, whether anybody asks or not, "Because it's there . . . because it's there . . ."

But I would like to sustain today, right here in this charming little book, that there are other sorts of adventures that are just as valid as those more overtly melodramatic types — and perhaps in the long run even more valid. These are the invitations to adventure that lie all about us and which go too long unnoticed, most often hidden in the guises of the comfortably homey and disguised in the subtle and often treacherous forms of what we THINK we know.

To give only one example, I once lived in a beautiful building, which had a quite extraordinary history. The man who had built it was one of the two wealthiest men in the city, and he built the building only for himself and his family. There were — and, as far as I know, are — hidden phonelines that link the apartments, special secret panels, and God knows what else! But the interesting thing was that not one person in that building had the spirit of adventure — and of discovery — to explore the enticing mysteries of what was there right under us and, indeed, all around us.

I mention these elements of adventure because I think this fascinating little book, by this unknown woman who was Marian Shaw, about the World's Fair that everyone THOUGHT they knew, is itself that kind of adventure. It is in itself a voyage into the unknown, but into the unknown, unbeknownst to us, right here with us (which, in truth, only makes it more delectable, like discovering that your husband can sing Grand Opera!). It is like suddenly finding something revealed by a voice one did not hear before.

First, the very manner of the finding of Marian Shaw's manuscript was in itself an adventure — to discover this scrapbook of her lost articles, with her spidery handwriting accompanying the old articles, is in itself a great adventure. Then, for the editors and publishers to have the literary sense to see that this is a little cache of historic riches demands on their part a real sense of literary adventure, indeed of the type that we see far too rarely in today's vulgar and unpleasing "bottom line" culture. Finally, to dig, and dig, and look around, and dig some more, and finally find out who was this forgotten and prolific woman, this forgotten naif, this Marian Shaw, woman writer when there were none — well, that took a great physical and intellectual sense of adventure.

And, finally, all of these little acts of courage, in the service of curiosity, adding up to unearthing and finally publishing these wonderfully rich, evocative, and descriptive articles. They then proceed to tell us, as nothing else, what the great World's Fair (the epic of the achievements of our time) truly meant to its awakening world.

But *World's Fair Notes* is more than that. It is the kind of book that will be extremely valuable for students of journalism, for women's studies, and for general history. Its lasting importance lies in the fact that, almost exactly one hundred years later, this book gives us a rare and until now hidden look into a woman and into a great historic event which in its time exemplified "man's" highest hopes and dreams.

We must also understand that these excellent articles remained hidden for so long precisely because women simply were to be "seen" but not heard; they were surely not to be "seen" through the revelation of their spirit and will, which is always and ever expressed above all in writing. Yet, Marian Shaw, and in the next years, more and more courageous and self-willed women refused that definition of themselves, as they insisted not only upon looking at their world but defining it through their own observations and images and thoughts.

Chicago, the city where I was born and raised and a city I dearly love, holds a special place in terms of the development of women's definition of their worlds. Chicago's is a rough and ready history, home of the Italian Mafia, haven of corrupt ward-heelers and venue of the infamous St. Valentine's Day Massacre. But Chicago was also home to an extraordinary march of women across the trajectory of its unique history. Ironically, these women were mostly aristocrats, but they were also tough ladies with a street sense that guaranteed their acts.

Right in the trail of Marian Shaw, and exemplifying women in Chicago history, came the great Jane Addams, who went to the poorest and most dangerous area of Chicago, founded the first settlement house there, and put the name of Hull House into social work history, not to speak of the names of such stellar women as Ellen Gates Starr, Judith Lathrop, Florence Kelley, Grace and Edith Abbott, and Jessie Binford.

But Chicago and American journalism did not easily or swiftly change. Women writers moved into the newsrooms of the big Chicago papers during

World War II and did exceedingly well; but when the war ended and the men came home, they were moved out just as quickly.

By the time I came to the Chicago *Daily News*, in 1959, to start on the society page, the managing editor told me without the slightest hesitation or embarrassment, as regards getting into the news room, that "we have a quota of two women for the news room. One does education and one does 'sob stories.' There have always been two women — and there always will be two women."

I hated to be disruptive, but the next year I became the "third woman." Those were wonderful years, even though our editors had a distinct propensity to send Lois Wille, our brilliant writer, later to win two Pulitzer Prizes, out on "our girl" stories. This could be anything from Lois' brushing a hippopotamus's teeth (the hippo, as you might expect, wasn't keen on it) to my driving a sulky around the racetrack and masquerading as a waitress at a big Mafia wedding (neither the sulky nor the Mafia were very keen on that, either.)

Four years later, in 1964, I went overseas for the *Daily News* and became the first and for a long time only woman foreign correspondent in the country. In those years, indeed, my paper opened up totally to women, as did all papers. The men, I must add, were wonderful to us; we were a tight little journalistic band of brothers and a few sisters, and Chicago journalism was so much fun that it should have been immoral (some of it, like looking through transoms for stories, was already close to illegal).

At any rate, today there are so many women in journalism that, whenever I look into one of the formerly closed city rooms, I often see that more than half the reporters now are women. This trend has not proceeded as rapidly to the editor levels, but there are also some high-ranking women editors. There are fewer women foreign correspondents that one would suppose, but this is no longer because the field is not open; it is because women tend to go overseas for two or three years, do well, and then return home to get married or go into an editor's job. I am one of the insane ones who has stayed out there, travelling around and seeking out St. Exupery's romantic "accidents of journeying."

During my own odd professional trajectory, I worked everywhere in the world. Marian Shaw, on the other hand, stayed in her own milieu, in her own society, but chose to cover — and to cover with the most definite intensity that shows in her passionate descriptions and loving images — a "World's Fair," which of course is a representation of all of the world. So, yes, we were sisters; I think I would have liked to know this woman of such cultured taste, who emerged from nowhere out of one meager year in a frontier teachers' school!

Finally, the related questions that constantly worried me, with all their thickets of dangers during the years, remain still unanswered to me. That pride of questions is: "Do women bring different qualities — something qualitative and culturally and spiritually different — to their writing, and to public life? Does it ultimately matter whether woman's voice is heard?"

I find that, to be truthful, I cannot answer those questions yet. We still don't have enough of a sampling, and many professional women journalists today seem only to ape men's writing, and too often the worst men's writing. But here, in this unique and mellow little book, so filled with an almost girlish unspoiled enthusiasm, we have a kind of fresh, pure, unsullied example of an obviously very intelligent and sensitive woman's view of an important moment in time. It makes you wish you could walk around the Columbian Exposition with a curious adventurer and guide named Marian Shaw.

GEORGIE ANNE GEYER
WASHINGTON, D.C.
JUNE 14, 1992

World's Fair Notes

THE WORLD'S FAIR

A Special Correspondent Tells
of the Many Beauties to Be
Seen There.

Pen Portrayal of Some of the
Scenes and Incidents
During a Visit.

Valuable Advice Will Be Found
by Those Intending Visiting
the Fair.

CHICAGO, Aug. 18.—[Special Correspondence.]—In a letter of Bishop Vincent, written upon the occasion of his first visit to the Holy Land, he says: "I said to my friend, just before landing at Joppa, 'when our feet touch the sacred soil, let our first words and thoughts be those of praise and devotion!' A moment after, we were standing in the muddiest and filthiest spot I had ever seen, among yelling Arabs, howling muleteers, braying donkeys and sights and sounds more suggestive of the inferno than of the hallowed, peaceful Canaan of our dreams, and our first impulse was to curse rather than to pray."

The visitor at the world's fair who enters from the land side is liable to experience a similar, though less poignant, disappointment. We had expected the glorious panorama of the "White City of the Unsalted Sea," with its glittering domes and towers to burst upon our vision like a thing of beauty. After pushing our way through noisy crowds of street vendors, hackmen and rumbling carts, deafened by the roar of the elevated trains above our heads, we entered the gates of our long-looked for Elysium. The roar of the outside world, indeed, had died away, and the peace and quiet within the walls was a blissful contrast to the Babel outside, but as sightseers we were disappointed. Nothing more attractive than the rear of some of the state buildings met our eyes. To the left, upon a raised platform, a savage looking grizzly bear, standing upon his hind legs, grimly invited us to enter the Esquimaux village. Doubtless the ethnological student finds here much to interest him, but it would be well for all visitors to this primitive encampment to follow the example of the Cossacks when they attacked the garlic-eating French battallion—stop their nostrils with clay. One finds here as many odors as Coleridge found in the unfragrant city of Cologne—"all well defined." Emerging into the fresh air again, we take in a few whiffs of pure oxygen, and continue our walk. Now we begin to be repaid. A broad, beautiful avenue opens before us, at the further extremity of which we catch a glimpse of the waters of Lake Michigan, "darkly, deeply, beautifully blue." On either side of this avenue lie the state buildings, varying in style of architecture as well as in external and internal decoration. Some of these buildings serve merely as headquarters for the commissioners from the various states, and are not distinctive in any way, having comfortable and restful, often elegant salons and waitingrooms for the convenience of visitors. The most interesting are those which in their architecture and decoration are illustrative of the peculiar industries or products of the states they represent.

Loyal North Dakotans will not fail to visit their beautiful building, for the erection of which the generous contributions of private citizens exceeded the $50,000 appropriated by the legislature. They will feel a just pride not only in the wonderful exhibit of the resources and industries of their young state, but in the artistic arrangement of the native products which adds greatly to their attractiveness. Those unexperienced in this form of decoration would never imagine that the simple products of the field could be woven into such fantastic and beautiful forms as are found in the decorations of many of the western states. Notable among these are the pavilions of grains and native grasses found in the exhibits of Kansas, Illinois, the two Dakotas, Colorado and Iowa. Art in this direction reaches perhaps its culminating point in the Iowa building, where is found the wonderful "corn palace" formed entirely of grain artistically arranged in frescoes, arches, columns, friezes and pavilions. There are bas-reliefs of agricultural designs done in grass and grains, fantastic forms, graceful scroll work, mythological figures, monuments and statues entirely composed of grains of corn, wheat, oats and various kinds of seeds. The only agricultural product which the artist has failed to make use of is the poor homely potato. Here also in miniature is a model of the state house done in grains and seeds, its noble porticos and columns formed of different colored grains in glass tubes and receptacles of various shapes. The "flax palace" is another unique structure composed of flax in different stages of growth and development.

One of the most original and interesting of the state buildings is that of Idaho. It is built of immense native logs to represent the rude home of the western pioneer. Its windows, panels, and wainscoting are made of native ore covered with mica of which Idaho is said to produce the finest quality in the world.

Within, the building is furnished in true pioneer style, most of the massive, furniture being home made, artistically adorned with stag horns and deer skins. Buffalo and wolf skins take the place of carpets, and the walls are adorned with trophies of the chase, hunters' equipments, and Indian curiosities. A few articles of luxury are seen, reminiscences of the comfort which the pioneer has left behind him in his far-distant eastern home. In this building also is to be found the mica hall, and many beautiful specimens of agates.

California attracts the visitor again and again. The building is a mixture of the old adobe mission house, with something of the ornate Moorish to relieve the somber effect. On its roof is a tropical garden, above which rises a dome eighty feet in height. In some of its towers swing the old Spanish bells that in early times called the devout pioneer to worship. Within the building is a bewildering display of fruits, grains, tropical plants, minerals and other products of this wonderful state. A short distance from the entrance a bronze statue of James Marshall, the discoverer of gold, confronts us. Dressed in a rough miner's suit, with broad brimmed, slouch hat, he stands erect holding in his right hand a nugget of gold, with his left hand pointing to the place of its discovery. A little further down the main aisle is a figure of a horse and rider in knight's armor, with coat of mail and helmet, holding a sword in his outstretched hands. This unique figure is made entirely of prunes and at a distance the effect is striking. A noble statue of the state of California adorns the central aisle, a heroic female figure holding an olive branch in her right hand, her left arm embracing the national flag and the hand resting upon a shield bearing the emblem of the state.

In the Colorado building may be seen Powers' famous statue, "The Last of His Race," bought for $10,000 by the enterprising women of Colorado. Native marble, minerals and wood have entered into the construction of this building. The columns are adorned with native grains and grasses, and there are a series of friezes and pictures wrought in colored grains.

Florida is represented by a reproduction of "Old Fort Marion," the oldest structure in America. Its exhibit consists of flowers, fruits, sponges, corals, sea shells, while all around are palmettos and other tropical plants. In this building the famous "butter sculptress," Caroline Shawk Brooks, has her studio, and we were favored with an interview with this remarkable and talented woman. She has on exhibition many fine pieces of sculpture, of which perhaps the "Sleeping Iolanthe," "Lady Godiva," and "Love's Dream," in the Missouri building, are the most beautiful. From her earliest childhood she has modeled in clay or what ever plastic material came to her hand. At 7 years of age she molded blue clay from the spring near her father's house, a portrait of Dante, copied from the cover of an old book belonging to her father. After her marriage she moved onto a farm in Missouri, and there found an outlet for her genius in molding the butter which she prepared for market into fanciful and beautiful forms. She always models in butter, as she finds this medium more plastic and sympathetic than clay. Her works are afterwards put into plaster and marble. She has never had any instruction, but in her travels abroad has been enabled to observe the works of great masters, and thereby improve her own.

In Louisiana we find a reproduction of an old plantation house, with its broad veranda, immense doors and quaint dormer windows, shaded by the mournful cypress with its funereal draperies of Spanish moss. Here are many curiosities and relics of old Creole days—a Creole kitchen and café. One room is constructed entirely of the beautiful curly pine. There are specimens of crystal salt from the famous Avery mine in New Iberia. One room is given up to "Evangeline's people," the only surviving remnants of the old Acadians whose sorrows have been so pathetically portrayed in Longfellow's immortal poem. Driven from their happy homes, these weary wanderers finally settled along the borders of the Bayou Têche in southwestern Louisiana. Here they have since lived. By intermarriage with the Indians they have greatly deteriorated, the men being lazy and worthless. The women, however, are industrious and frugal. Their chief industry is the weaving of a cloth of peculiar texture from the native nankeen cotton, which, as its name indicates, is of a yellowish hue. They have also a secret method of dyeing a certain fadeless blue. And the processes of carding, spinning and weaving are shown in their quarters here.

At the entrance of the Minnesota state building stands the beautiful Hiawatha statue, contributed by the school children of the state. It represents Hiawatha bearing the lovely Minnehaha in his arms "over lakes and streams and rivers." It was designed by Fjelde, a Norwegian sculptor, of Minneapolis. The Minnehaha window in one of the parlors forms another attraction. Over the stairway is a unique chandelier, formed by the union of three stags' heads, from each of whose branching antlers hangs a bulb sparkling with incandescent light.

Three territories, New Mexico, Arizona and Oklahoma, have erected for joint use a beautiful little building, with

The Minnesota State Building

"At the entrance to the Minnesota state building stands the beautiful
Hiawatha statue, contributed by the school children of the state."

a roof garden, and containing specimens of all the flora of the three territories. It has a fine archeological exhibit,
and rare old Spanish paintings on elk
skin, some of which are over 600 years
old.

Before the Utah building stands a
bronze statue of Brigham Young, the
patron saint of the Mormons. This statue does not seem to meet with much
favor, and most of the passersby deign
it only a glance, usually of disapproval.
Within the building are beautiful
exhibits of gold, silver, sulphur, silk and
the various industries of the state. A
miniature reproduction of Great Salt
Lake is an attractive feature.

Virginia is represented by an exact
fac-simile of the Mount Vernon home of
George Washington. It contains many of
the originals, and, where these could

not be obtained, the duplicates of the
contents of this American Mecca, consisting of antique furniture, silverware,
old paintings and hangings. Among
other curiosities are some paintings and
embroideries done by Nellie Custis, an
old harpsichord belonging also to her,
presented by George Washington. Little
hatchets, supposed to represent the
mythological implement owned by
truthful George, are here offered for
sale.

In most of the buildings of the southern and New England states the colonial
style of architecture prevails, and in all
of them one finds interesting relics of
old colonial days. Perhaps the most
attractive of these is the Connecticut
building. All the rooms are furnished in
the style of 100 or 200 years ago. In
some, the walls are covered with silk

18

tapestry, fac-similes of that which adorned the walls in the mansion of some colonial magnate. Others are decorated with paper in bright pictorial designs of animals, birds and flowers, such as never were seen "in heaven above, on the earth beneath, or in the waters under the earth." There is the gun with which Gen. Israel Putnam shot the wolf, the chair of "Parson Newell" 1630, a high-posted bed-stead of mahogany 250 years old, with embroidered quilt, curtains and valance from 100 to 200 years old. The bed is so high that steps are necessary to climb up to it. There are chintz covered chairs of 1740, spindle-legged tables, massive mahogany bureaus with brass mountings, old clocks which have steadily ticked away the lives of five or six generations—rugs braided by hands that have "lain for a century dead." In corner cupboards taken from some of the earliest houses in Connecticut are to be seen antique china with fanciful and startling designs, silver spoons, ewers, and tankards, and various cooking utensils of a fashion long since forgotten. In glass cases are preserved relics of old embroidery, wedding finery of our great-great grandmothers, infants' clothing, caps and christening robes in which the babies of generations past toddled and crept and wailed, and ancient dolls that were fondled by little maidens of the seventeenth century. On the walls hang silhouettes and colored prints, mourning pieces representing some sorrow-stricken woman bending over a tombstone on which are inscribed the virtues of the dear departed, the landscape bright with startling greens and variegated flowers whose coloring might well make Dame Nature pale with envy. Beside the great fireplaces with their ancient cranes, are old-fashioned bellows, shovel and tongs, and in a convenient place near by hangs

the useful, time-honored warming-pan. In one of the sweet, old-fashioned parlors is a spinet of five octaves made in London, 1725, bearing above its keyboard the inscription "sollicitae jucunda oblivio vitae," which may be freely translated "sweet forgetfulness of the cares of life." There are samplers most elaborate in design and wonderful in execution, wrought by industrious little hands that have long since gone to their reward. One done in 1734 by Sarah Ann Eliot—descendant of the great Indian apostle—"in the ninth year of her age at Miss Kimberl's school," recounts in cross-stitch the virtues of some departed relative. We would fain have lingered in this quaint and quiet spot, which seemed to us a sort of "saint's rest." We felt as though transported to another world far-removed from the strife and turmoil of our hurrying, bustling nineteenth century.

In the New Hampshire building we found more relics, revolutionary and pre-revolutionary. Here are views of the White Mountains, a panoramic view of the Pemagewasset river, and a beautiful grotto combining the beauties and wonders of many similar grottos of the "Old Granite State."

In the New England group, "Little Rhody" is represented by a beautiful building of the Doric order, filled with relics and objects of interest. It is among the most attractive of this group, and has been presented to the City of Chicago.

Texas, the "Lone Star" state, is represented by a building constructed after the style of the old Spanish mission. It contains special exhibits of great value and thousands of curiosities and relics.

Ohio has an elegant building, partly colonial, partly modern, with rich and costly decorations. One of its greatest attractions is the monument in front of the main entrance, typifying the great-

Farm scene in the Illinois State Building
"The varied and profuse exhibit of Illinois fills its magnificent
building from floor to dome."

ness of the state. It represents "Ohio" in the form of Cornelia, a graceful and noble bronze figure standing upon a granite pedestal. At her feet, surrounding the base of the monument are statues, also in bronze of six statesmen, Sheridan, Grant, Sherman, Chase, Stanton and Garfield towards whom she points, while above them the carved inscription, "These are my jewels," fully expresses Ohio's pride in her sons.

At the entrance of Missouri's building stands the beautiful marble statue "Love's Dream" already referred to. It represents a half length female figure rising from a shell, a cupid clinging to her breast. Water lilies and cupids riding on dolphins surround the base. The faces are pure and classic. The beautiful "jasper room," whose walls sparkle with crude lead and zinc next attracts us. This room was furnished and decorated by the women of Jasper county. Other rooms fitted up with modern elegance testify to the enterprise of various cities of the state.

The varied and profuse exhibit of Illinois fills its magnificent building from floor to dome. The sightly yellow dome of this building, visible from nearly every part of the grounds, soon becomes a familiar landmark. Entering on the north side, one pauses to gaze on the tattered battle flags that tell in a

20

silence more eloquent than words of the part Illinois' brave sons took in the preservation of the union. Many relics of early days are found here, among them the church bell that first awakened the resounding echoes of the Mississippi valley. It was presented by Louis XV to Marquette. We should linger too long if we attempted to examine all that art, science, literature and agriculture have contributed to these spacious halls. We pass on to Indiana, attracted by its red Gothic towers and gray walls, and linger to recline a while in the comfortable *chaises longues* in the cosiest of its many charming salons.

Kentucky typifies in its structure a southern colonial mansion, filled with interesting relics and curiosities, while its cool parlors and verandas tempt the weary sight-seer to repose.

Maine shows many relics and historic treasures. A group of stuffed animals will interest the zoologist. Maryland has fitted up an elegant club house. Its special exhibits are to be found in the main buildings. In the chaste and elegant Grand Rapids and Saginaw rooms of the Michigan building, one is fain to linger and listen to the soul-filling strains of the grand organ, which, at night, illuminated by 500 incandescent lamps, delights both eyes and ears. The Grand Rapids room is in Louis XIV style, in white and gold with old colonial fire place. The walls are everywhere adorned with exquisite tapestries and paintings.

The Montana building, noted for originality of design, is filled with products, chiefly mineral, peculiar to the state. Before the Washington building rises a stately flagstaff of native fir, 250 feet high. At its base is a pyramid of the various mineral products of the state. Within the building we see a miniature representation of a harvest scene where are shown all the processes of plough-ing, planting, harvesting and threshing. There is also an interesting educational exhibit.

In Kansas, aside from the agricultural exhibit, is a collection, arranged with panoramic effect, of North American mammals. This exhibit is furnished by the State university. A miniature train of cars, illustrative of the Kansas & Topeka railroad, whizzes above our heads around the circuit of the galleries.

Nebraska's headquarters are commodious and elegant, with many interesting special exhibits. Like many of the western buildings, it is fragrant with the sweet perfume of the harvest fields. New Jersey presents a fac-simile of Washington's headquarters at Morristown, with many relics of revolutionary times, and exhibits of the products and industries of the state.

Probably the most substantial building on the exposition grounds is that of Wisconsin. It is constructed of brown stone from the shores of Lake Superior, pressed brick from Menominee, and shingles from the woods of its northern forests. Its interior is beautifully finished in hard wood and mosaics, and all its material, except the onyx finishing, is derived from its own state. There are few characteristic exhibits, but two beautiful works of art deserve special mention. One illustrates the motto of the state, "Forward." A graceful female figure stands in the prow of a boat whose figurehead is Old Abe, the famous eagle of the Eighth Wisconsin regiment. The left hand grasps a flag, while the right is extended upward and forward. The face is expressive of energy and determination, without sacrificing any of the "eternal womanly." The figure was designed by Miss Miner of Madison. The other statue represents the "Genius of Wisconsin." It is a female figure of exquisite contour and graceful pose. She leans against a rock with the head slightly thrown back, displaying the exquisite mouldings of throat and neck. The left arm is raised, with the hand resting caressingly upon the neck of an eagle with lowered beak and extended wings. The face of the woman expresses nobility, purity and sweetness. The left hand hangs lightly at her side. The drapery falls in graceful folds from the right shoulder, leaving the left arm, breast and shoulder bare. This statue is the work of Miss Nellie Farnsworth Meers of Oshkosh. She is not yet 21 years of age, and has received no instruction. From a child, she has always had a mania for modelling. After her model has been accepted by the judges she was advised to study under some efficient art instructor, but her teachers soon decided to leave her genius to its own bent, and allow her to work in her own way, with her own tools. The statue described above has been pronounced by eminent surgeons to be anatomically perfect, and Julian Hawthorne declares it to be the finest thing in art on the exposition grounds. Miss Meers is one of three gifted sisters, specimens of whose work in art and literature are to be found in the woman's department.

The Old Bay state is fittingly represented by a mansion modeled after the old Hancock house, for many years a familiar landmark on Beacon street, Boston. It is furnished with old-time elegance and contains many ancient and historic relics, and notable works of art. Here are copies of the charters granted by King Charles and William and Mary, old state papers, rare old portraits, glass cases containing the rich brocades and wedding finery of old-time belles, who doubtless caused many a heart-throb and pang of jealousy in the breasts of ancient cavaliers who flourished in those days "when we lived under the king"—embroidered wedding slippers of a very substantial size, testifying to the broad understanding of our feminine ancestors. There is a cradle in which five generations of the Adams family, including the two presidents, have been rocked, (this cradle was made by the village undertaker) autograph letters of noted authors, poets and statesmen, solemn antiquities and other things too numerous to mention. A unique embroidered sampler, done by Mary Parsons, aged 10, in 1740, represents Adam and Eve in the Garden of Eden. The conception is so original and so different from the usually accepted idea of our first parents in their primitive state, that it is well worth studying. "Under green apple boughs," laden with the reddest specimens of the fruit of that forbidden tree which "brought death into the world, and all our woes," are seated a lady and gentleman dressed in the height of the prevailing fashion of a century and a half ago—a style wonderfully in advance of the traditional fig leaf. Adam, attired in a red and yellow skirted coat, with a ruff, knee breeches, high heeled, silver-buckled shoes, and powdered wig, looks benignly down upon Eve, seated a little below him on the flowery bank. From under the ample skirts of the lady peeps coquettishly the toe of a slipper. A long pointed waist, flowing sleeves, and elaborate headdress complete our primal mother's costume. An impossible parrot is perched upon her knee, while all around are nondescript animals whose like has never been seen since the fall, if indeed they existed before. Eve is languidly reaching up for the fatal fruit, serenely unconscious of all the mischief she is brewing.

The "Keystone State" has reproduced in part Independence Hall. This building also has been presented to the city of Chicago. It is spacious and elegant, adorned with beautiful frescoes, stained glass windows, painting and tapestries. Among the many relics found here is the old "Liberty Bell" with its famous inscription "Proclaim liberty throughout all the land, to all the inhabitants thereof." Here is the chair in which Jefferson sat when he wrote the Declaration of Independence, and the inkstand which he used on that occasion, the charter given to Penn by Charles II, and many portraits of historic characters.

Probably the most magnificent of all the state buildings is that of New York—the "Empire State." It fittingly represents in its mosaic, marble floors, its broad and richly ornamented stairway, its marble fountains, elegant banquet hall and salons, the wealth and magnificence of the greatest state in the union. This beautiful structure is, in part, a reproduction of the old Van Rensselaer residence, for many years a familiar historic landmark of New York city. Here also are many interesting relics of the old Dutch colonists, descending from the time of rough old Peter Stuyvesant through the Knickerbockers and all the famous "Vans" that have helped to make the history and prosperity of the state. From the roof of this building we obtained our first extended view of the fair grounds. Whatever feeling of disappointment we may have experienced at our first entrance, all was forgotten in the glorious prospect spread out before us. To the east was the shoreless lake in all its blue expanse, to the north and west lay the great, busy city of Chicago, whose turmoil reached us only in the faintest echoes, while to the south, the "White City" was unfolded in all its marvelous beauty. Its minarets, domes and towers were lighted up by the clear sunlight. Its peaceful lagoons with gondolas darting hither and thither, and the cool retreats of "Wooded Island" added an indescribable charm. No sound of traffic or labor disturbed the quietness of the scene. But for the crowd of pleasure-seekers wandering through the broad avenues, we could scarcely have realized that it was a city of the living. We recalled the words of Rev. Mr. Stead in a recent article in the *Review of Reviews*, that never, until he reaches the New Jerusalem, does he expect to look upon a scene of such bewildering beauty.

Let no one who visits the world's fair fail to spend a day at least in making a tour of the state buildings. Here will be found something to suit the tastes of all. The student of history, the romancist, the scientist, the geologist, the lover of nature, can revel in those things which most delight his soul. Nowhere else can one gain so clear an idea of the progress and prosperity of our country, and of its marvelous resources. The heart of the loyal American thrills with pride as he gazes upon these evidences of our country's greatness. The more he investigates and examines, the more assured he will be that,

"This is the land, of every land the pride,
Beloved by heaven, o'er all the world beside."

MARIAN SHAW.

23

The Yerkes Telescope in the Liberal Arts and Manufactures Building

"Beginning with the cliff dwellers and other primitive races, one can trace the progress of mankind in all stages of civilization and barbarism until he reaches the wonderful works of the nineteenth century."

THE WORLD'S FAIR

Marian Shaw Favors The Argus With Another Grist of World's Fair News.

A Trip Over the Intramural Road One That Should Be Taken by Visitors.

From This Elevated and Ever Changing Point of View Sights Are Entrancing.

A Visit to the Anthropological Building Not to Be Missed by Students of Ethnology.

CHICAGO, Aug. 26—[Special Correspondence.]—The extreme opposite part of Jackson park from that in which the state buildings are situated is today our objective point. Taking the Intramural train near the Fifty-ninth street entrance, borne above the heads of the crowd, we make a rapid circuit of the western and southern portion of the grounds to the south loop. From our elevated and ever-changing point of view, we look down upon the broad avenues, filled, even at this early hour, with sight-seers, and the marble like palaces interspersed with here and there a structure of darker stone. The glittering glass dome of the Palace of Horticulture first attracts us; then the massive Transportation Building with its curious and ornate decoration. To the right, a little further on, lie the blackened ruins of the Cold Storage Building, mournful reminders of the tragedy that so recently sent a thrill of horror throughout the land. Past Machinery Hall and the Palace of Agriculture we are whirled, catching occasional glimpses of the lagoon and Grand Basin, and lastly of the great lake itself, so like the ocean that we miss nothing but the saltiness. Our delightful and exhilarating ride comes to an end all too soon, and we alight and look around us. Here, in this southern corner of the grounds, is much to interest the sight-seer, whatever his tastes may be. The student of ethnology may wander for hours through the halls of the anthropological building studying man and his works, as here illustrated from pre-historic times down to the present. Beginning with the cliff dwellers and other primitive races, one can trace the progress of mankind in all stages of civilization and barbarism through the ages until he reaches the wonderful works of the nineteenth century. Here are found implements, ornaments and utensils used by the human family thousands of years ago—skeletons of men and animals belonging to races now for ages extinct—ruins of ancient temples with idols and other sacred relics. The progress of art may be traced from the rude picture writing and sculpture of the primitive races, as displayed in the totem poles of the British American Indian, the stone carvings and hieroglyphics on the ruins of ancient Egyptian, Assyrian and Aztec temples, down to the bold and beautiful creations of Phidias and Michael Angelo, and the exquisite works of modern painters and sculptors found in every nook and corner of the exposition grounds. The casual observer gazes for a moment with curiosity and amusement at the ugly carved monstrosities and the queer tracery upon the stones of the ruins of Guatemala, Copan and

Honduras, but the archeologist treasures every stone and line, anxiously awaiting the day when the key to these hieroglyphics shall be found, and he can open to the world these sealed pages of history. We give one shuddering glance at the horrors of the Peruvian burial ground, pause a few moments to gaze at the motley collection of curiosities from South Wales, and pay our respects to "Mickey," the once valiant king of the Ulladullaas, chief of the cannibals and victor in eighty fatal contests. This doughty warrior, who celebrated his victories by devouring the hearts of his vanquished foes, at last came under the humanizing influences of Christian missionaries, abandoned his career of bloodshed, put himself upon a more simple diet; laid down his boomerang and war club, and devoted himself to religion and art. He has painted several pictures of the primitive life of his people, some of which are on exhibition. Two years ago he died in the odor of sanctity at the age of 80 years.

In this building there are also to be found interesting exhibits by the bureau of hygiene and sanitation, charities and correction. Outside the building, but connected with this department, are living representatives of various Indian tribes, living as their forefathers did before the white man invaded these shores. Here in their wigwams or bark huts they cook and sleep, carry on their games and dances. Among the tribes represented are the Crees, Chippewas, Sioux, Winnebagos, Iroquois, Choctaws, Apaches and Papagos. South America is represented by the Arrawaks and Bolivians. Among the latter is found the largest man in the world, being 9 feet 10 inches in height and weighing 418 pounds. It is but a step from these dwellings of the aborigines to the convent of La Rabida, once the asylum of the great discoverer whose voyage across the Atlantic sealed the fate of the red man and opened to the white man a new world. It was at the Spanish convent of La Rabida that, four centuries ago, Columbus, footworn, weary and famished, applied for rest and food. The good prior, Father de Marchena, not only received him kindly, but listened with interest to his plans of exploration, and secured him a reception at the court of Ferdinand and Isabella. The quaint structure we see before us is a facsimile of the ancient convent. It is filled with valuable relics of Columbus—manuscripts, autograph letters and copies of the earliest books relating to America, with quaint maps and charts of the newly discovered country. Here is a church bell taken from the famous mosque of the Alhambra by Queen Isabella and presented to Columbus. It was brought by him to America and presented to a community of monks. After many vicissitudes it at last found a resting place in the tower of a little negro church at Haleyville, N.J. Six roughly hewn blocks of stone show all that now remains of the first Christian church on the western hemisphere. Among the curios displayed here are gold coins made from the first gold found in America, a collection from the Vatican, sent here by his holiness, the pope. Some relics of the discovery of America by the Norsemen are likewise exhibited, including early published volumes relating to that discovery, and a fac-simile of the inscription on Dighton Rock, said to have been carved by the Norsemen in the tenth century. There is a portrait of Leif Ericsson and also one of Kublai Khan, who is said to have visited America in the thirteenth century.

Leaving this depository of historic relics, we pause to gaze a few moments at the "Viking Ship" anchored near by, an exact reproduction of the old Norse

The Krupp Gun Works

"When science, art and human skill have all combined to produce such death-dealing monsters as these Krupp guns, one naturally feels that the millenium is far off, and that the time is not yet when 'spears shall be beaten into plow shares and swords into pruning hooks.'"

vessels of a thousand years ago, and a fac-simile of the one in which Leif Ericsson sailed to the North American shores. Moored side by side with these are the Santa Maria, Pinta and Nina, built by the Spanish government after exact measurement and models, and believed to be true representations of that historic fleet in which Columbus made his immortal voyage. Compared with our present ocean vessels and steamers, these ships seem mere toys, and we marvel at the courage that dared venture in such crafts as these over an unknown and trackless sea, and we re-read with renewed interest the history of those ninety days of peril.

With reluctance we leave these relics and records of antiquity, with their halo of olden romance, and memories of a civilization long past, and rubbing our eyes as though wakened from a Rip Van-Winkle sleep, are transported in body and spirit to the realities of the nineteenth century. Before us stands an imposing building resembling an old feudal castle, with turrets and towers, from each of which protrudes a threatening cannon. But as our mission is one of peace, we enter without fear. On every side are vast glittering engines of destruction, and in their midst, occupying the position of honor looms the gigantic form of "Krupp's Baby," as it is called—a monster gun, the largest and most powerful ever cast, weighing 127 tons and having a range of sixteen miles. Huge steel targets eighteen inches thick are shown which have been penetrated by balls from this immense piece of ordinance. From breach to muzzle this, the biggest cannon of the world, measures 57 feet, the diameter of its yawning, murderous mouth is $16\frac{2}{3}$ inches. A single load for this leviathan costs $1,100. The carriage on which it rests is built of steel. It is approached by steps and is so arranged with cog-wheels and levers that it can be easily raised or lowered, and turned in any direction. This gun has been presented to Chicago and will remain when the fair closes. When science, art and human skill have all combined to produce such death-dealing monsters as these Krupp guns, one naturally feels that the millenium is far off, and that the time is not yet when "spears shall be beaten into plow shares and swords into pruning hooks." But it may be that these mighty machines will in reality hasten the day when there shall be "neither wars nor rumors of war." If this be so, all hail to "Krupp's Baby"—the herald of peace!

In the shoe and leather building we find nothing to shock our sensibilities or to arouse our warlike proclivities. All is serene and peaceful. We see leather here in all its forms, from its primitive and natural use as it serves to protect or adorn the denizen of the forest and the farmyard, to the dainty glove or slipper designed for the belle of the ballroom, or the soft little shoe of the wee toddler who has just started out on the weari-

some journey of life. Carriage tops, upholstered chairs and lounges, harness, saddles, belting and a hundred other articles made of leather are here shown. Improved machinery in the manufacture of leather goods is exhibited and one may watch the process from the raw hide to the finished shoe. Give your order for a pair of shoes, and fifteen minutes after the knife has entered the uncut leather, presto!—there they are! Rubber goods of every variety are also displayed here. There is a tanned elephant's hide weighing over 500 pounds. It was three years in the process of tanning. A tanned horse hide with head, mane and tail is another curiosity. An alligator's hide tanned with the head measures thirteen and a quarter feet, and a goatskin water bag is exhibited, which has seen eighty years service in Jerusalem. There is a belt twelve feet wide, capable of transmitting 5,000 horsepower, and a twelve inch belt 10,000 feet long. The pavilions of the leading shoe manufacturers are artistically arranged with luxurious chairs and couches upon which we were glad to recline after our wanderings and dream of the wonderful things we had seen. We had traced the progress of mankind by his works down through centuries of past time, but imagination failed to picture the future. Yet—"We doubt not through the ages, one increasing purpose runs, and the thoughts of men are widened with the process of the suns."

The Palace of Forestry is one of the most unique of all the exposition buildings. All around the building, whose dimensions are 208 by 528 feet, is a veranda whose roof is supported by a series of columns composed of tree trunks each 25 feet in length. All of these are left in their natural state with the bark intact, and are contributed by the various states and territories and by many foreign countries. The sides of the building are constructed of slabs with the bark removed. No iron enters into the construction of this building. Wooden pins take the place of bolts and bars. The main aisle is elaborately adorned with different kinds of woods. The roof is thatched with tanbark and other barks. The building contains a varied exhibition of forest products in all stages of growth and finish. There are dyewoods, mosses, lichens, abnormal growths, vegetable products used for bedding, gums, resins, vegetable ivory, and, in short, every thing of a woody nature that grows, and also many manufactured articles. Immense tree trunks are shown with one side left in its natural state, another rough-hewn and the third highly polished, displaying the beautiful grain of the wood. The odors of camphor and sandal-wood are mingled with the fragrance of the pine and cedar, and call to mind that line of the old missionary hymn that tells of "the spicy breezes" that "blow soft o'er Ceylon's isle." We gaze in awe at the fallen monarchs of the forest, one of which is said to have defied the winds and storms of a thousand years. We wonder at the skill that has brought out from these gnarled trunks their hidden beauty, as we look upon the polished surfaces of red-wood, mahogany, rosewood and ebony. "There is an angel in the stone," said Michael Angelo, as he stood before a rough slab of marble. But it needed the creative hand of the sculptor to make the angel visible. So there are untold and unimagined beauties beneath the rough bark of these forest trees, and the artist's hand supplementing the woodman's ax, has brought them to sight and light. Unique and beautiful pavilions of many colored woods of varied grain are scattered here and there, illustrative of the finest products of different states and countries.

There is a cabin made of cork, a wigwam of bamboo woven into varied designs, manufactured articles, from rustic pails and tubs, to exquisitely carved mantels and doorways. One of the most beautiful carvings displayed here is the gateway of the royal palace of Bombay, done in teak wood. In the Japanese section are immense bamboo rods that might have served as fishing poles for that ancient giant hero of "Mother Goose," who—

"Baited his hook with a dragon's tail,
And sat on the shore and bobbed for a whale."

Siam displays a mammoth piece of teak wood, the largest ever exported. The great red-wood plank from Humboldt county, California, attracts universal attention, the tree from which it was hewn was thirty-five feet in diameter, and was supposed to have attained the age of 1,500 years. The entire height of the tree was 800 feet. The plank itself is the largest in the world, being sixteen feet five inches in width, twelve feet nine inches long, and five inches thick. There are wonderful exhibits from New South Wales, Argentine Republic, Russia, and other foreign nations. Nebraska, among the so-called treeless prairie states, makes an excellent display. Among the curiosities is the trunk of the first tree planted under the timber culture patent of 1877. This building illustrates in a wonderful manner the forestry wealth of the world, and surpasses any display of the kind ever before made.

In this part of the grounds are also to be found the dairy exhibit, a distillery, a pioneer log cabin, an exhibit of windmills, a model workingman's home and, anchored in the South Pond is the whaling bark "Progress," in which are gathered many interesting relics.

The weary and hungry traveler may now, if he wishes, refresh himself at the

"Great White Horse Inn," a slightly modified model of the English inn of that name, immortalized by Dickens in his "Pickwick Papers." As for ourselves, we have taken in all that our minds can assimilate in one day, and are now ready to turn our weary steps cityward.
MARIAN SHAW.

CHICAGO LETTER.

A Spicy Letter From Our Special Correspondent at the White City.

The Wonders of the White City Exhibits Are Graphically Described.

The Wonderful Display of Machinery—

CHICAGO, Aug. 30.—[Special Correspondence.]—Machinery Hall or the Palace of Mechanic Arts is an immense building, magnificent in architectural designs and exterior adornment. It covers sixteen acres. In each of the four corners is a domed pavilion with a grand stair-case. Outside of the main hall is a large annex devoted mainly to home exhibits. The statues and portraits with which the building is ornamented represent the mechanical works of great inventors. Figures of victory adorn the towers and pinnacles. The pediment has ten figures of science and six of inventors. Entering the building the whirr of wheels and the roar of machinery assails our ears. We stand in awe before these mighty engines that seem endowed with life and intelligence. Here are the most magnificent engines, boilers and pumps ever constructed.

Interior of Machinery Hall

"Entering the building the whirr of wheels and the roar of machinery assails our ears. We stand in awe before these mighty engines that seem endowed with life and intelligence."

Machinist's tools, trip-hammers for forging, wonderful machines for the manufacture of textile fabrics, for working stone, for preparing food, for printing, lithographing and photography abound. The corridors of Machinery Hall display everything in the way of mechanic art that the genius of man has devised. Modern methods of fighting fire are demonstrated in numerous fire engines, hose carts, escapes and chemical apparatus. Great Britain and Canada have an exhibit which fills one corridor of this great building from east to west. Germany follows closely in their wake, and Belgium, Russia, France, Spain, Sweden, Austria and Brazil vie with each other in this friendly international strife. The gross space occupied by foreign exhibits is 83,000 square feet. The inventor or machinist could spend days or even weeks in these halls in intelligent study and observation. To the thousands who, like ourselves, have little or no knowledge of the principles underlying all these wonderful works, this building seems like the mysterious abode of mighty but unseen spirits. The revolving of the great wheels, the pulsation of immense piston rods steadily measuring the heart throbs of monster engines exercise over us an irresistible fascination, and inspire us with a feeling almost of terror. We know not which to marvel at more, the giant forces which man has caught and chained and harnessed down with iron bands, or the man himself, so puny in comparison with the monster he has created, who, by the pressure of a finger or a turn of the hand, can control its every movement, or stop its laboring breath, so that it stands a dead, inert mass of iron and steel, like a Goliath vanquished by the hand of little David. Among some of the exhibits most interesting to the ordinary sight-seer are the cotton, woolen and silk looms, which are in full operation,

machines for making hooks and eyes, wood embossing machines, which produce wooden souvenir medals of the world's fair while you wait, paper manufactured from wood pulp, printing presses which turn out the morning and evening papers for sale on the fair grounds, a machine for sewing carpets, where the operator rides a velocipede for 100 feet and guides an electric motor, which sews a carpet as he moves along. There are also machines for sewing wool and leather with wire thread, a weighing machine which takes coffee from the hopper, fills one pound paper bags and seals them at the rate of several tons of coffee a day, another that takes paper from the rolls, cuts a tag, prints the label upon it, punches the eyelet and inserts the wire for fastening, another that viciously bites off nails from wire and puts a head on them "quicker than a wink." In the south annex is the power plant, where there are about forty-three steam engines having from 18,000 to 20,000 horse-power. For the power in Machinery Hall there are twelve engines representing about 3,000 horse power. One engine alone is nearly a third larger than the famous Corliss engine of 1876.

Passing through the colonnade, we enter the Palace of Agriculture, one of the most magnificent and beautiful structures of the exposition, both in regard to external and internal decoration. Scattered throughout the main vestibule are pieces of statuary illustrative of agricultural industry. The pavilions representing the various states of the union are designed with reference to displaying in most artistic forms the agricultural products of each. Many are constructed and adorned with grasses in a manner similar to those already described in the state buildings. Among the most beautiful of these are Illinois, Iowa, the two Dakotas, Pennsylvania and New Jersey. In the Pennsylvania pavilion is a reproduction of Liberty bell in wheat, oats and rye. It is hung in a beautiful temple of native products, surmounted by a cap of multi-colored beans. Keeping guard over North Dakota is a heroic female figure, whose graceful draperies are formed of wheat ears fringed with grasses. This figure, a sort of modern Ceres, is visible from the galleries in nearly every part of the building. A distinctive feature of the New Jersey pavilion is the effective arrangement of pine cones in decoration. All exhibits are so arranged as to give an idea of the variety and perfection of the farming products of the world, and art has so lent its aid that the homeliest products of farm and garden are wrought into pleasing forms. Foreign exhibits occupy a space ranging each from 1,000 to 15,000 square feet. In the southern corner of the main floor is represented the entire work of a modern Agricultural Experiment station, covering the whole field of experiment and research in everything pertaining to agriculture, horticulture, entomology, dairy and veterinary science. A unique exhibit by a Pennsylvania firm is a map of the United States made of pickles, in which the rivers and lakes are represented by vinegar, and the larger cities by spices. Not only native products in

North Dakota Exhibit in the Palace of Agriculture

"Keeping guard over North Dakota is a heroic female figure, whose
graceful draperies are formed of wheat ears
fringed with grasses."

every stage of growth and development are displayed here, but also manufactured articles from vegetable products, including breadstuffs, starch, sugar, spices, liquors and confectionery. Nay more, they even mix and cook various articles of diet before your face and eyes, and serve them to you piping hot, "without money and without price." By judicious management one can, in the course of an afternoon, make out a good square meal. Here a dish of breakfast food with cream, there one of Aunt Dinah's pancakes, hot from the griddle, a little further on a delicious muffin shortened with cottolene, your fill of soup, bovril and bouillon, a nice cup of cocoa, and to finish off, a glass of root beer. "Walk up, gentlemen and ladies! Walk up and help yourselves! Here it is, and not a cent to pay!"

A booth after the plan of an Egyptian temple contains an exhibit of a cigarette manufacturing firm of Cairo, Egypt. An old-fashioned rustic mill, with water-wheel and millstones, represents a Duluth milling firm. Entering this rude structure you will be shown a picture of their mill of today, in striking contrast with the primitive affair of twenty years ago. The chocolate exhibit of a New York firm contains beautiful statues of Venus, Minerva and Columbus, cast in chocolate. In the German exhibit we see a noble statue of "Germania," also wrought in chocolate, and the Menier company has a tower of the same material weighing fifty tons and valued at $40,000. The Cape of Good Hope displays a live Zulu boy, 6 feet 7 $\frac{1}{2}$ inches tall. Why he is exhibited here among agricultural products does not appear. Perhaps, like Topsy, he "growed." From Canada comes a mighty cheese (here is a chance for a pun, but we forbear) weighing 20,000 pounds. Wisconsin has a booth made of timber, New Hampshire exhibits a curious plow made and

used by Daniel Webster. A star-shaped pyramid of soap, resting on a thirteen sided base, on which are carved the names of the thirteen original states, is the exhibit of a well known soap firm. On the top of this pyramid is the statue of the woman who made the original "stars and stripes." A medieval castle with turret-like projections, in each of which a miniature statue of Ceres represents a cereal company. In the annex south of the main building is displayed farm machinery of every description, both ancient and modern. Comparing the improved machines of today with the primitive affairs used by our ancestors one may trace the progress of agricultural science from the earliest times. Among all the exhibits of the exposition, none is more pleasing than that contained in the Agricultural building. The objects displayed here are those in which all have a common interest, and which all can understand, and whose practical utility all can appreciate. Not only is the eye charmed by beauty of arrangement and harmony of color, but the perfume of fruits mingles with the fragrance of the harvest field and the odor of spices, and there is a freshness and sweetness pervading the atmosphere that one finds nowhere else.

After refreshing ourselves in the Casino café, and resting awhile in the elegant salon, we step out on to the movable sidewalk for a ride around the pier. The entire length of this sidewalk is 4,500 feet. When outward bound we obtain a magnificent view of the lake and enjoy the cool lake breeze. As we round the point at the end of the pier, the waterfront of the White city rises before us. The exposition, as seen from this pier, or from the steamer as one approaches it by water, presents a scene of marvelous beauty. Directly in front of us is the Peristyle, a Grecian colonnade consisting of forty-eight columns, twenty-four on each side of the water gate or Columbus porticus. These columns symbolize the states and territories. On each column is an allegorical figure fourteen feet in height. Below are the coats of arms of the different states with the name of each. The length of the colonnade is 234 feet. Surmounting the porticus is the Columbus quadriga, representing Columbus standing in a chariot drawn by four prancing horses. Each pair of horses is led by a female figure in graceful, floating draperies. Another "quadriga," which also stands above the porticus, represents a female herald in a chariot drawn by four horses, led by male youths, with a pair of outriders in the rear. On either side of the arch are figures representing the genius of discovery and navigation. On the right hand, a little in the background, stands the Palace of Manufactures and Liberal Arts, and on the left we see the colossal statues and dome of the Agricultural building, upon the highest point of which is poised the beautiful "Diana" of St. Gaudens. This golden figure, acting as a weather vane, is turned with every breath of wind.

The Music Hall at the northern end of the Peristyle is built after the Roman renaissance with some Grecian features.

We enter between Corinthian columns, through a broad loggia and under arched door-ways into the auditorium which is capable of seating 1,000 people. The sum of $500,000 has been subscribed by the Exposition management to cover the cost of music here and in Choral Hall. The permanent Columbian chorus numbers 2,500 members, and the orchestra 120.

We complete our day's wanderings by a walk along the lake-shore boulevard, and a visit to the battle-ship Illinois, which is just south of the north pier. It is erected on piling, the water being too shallow to allow a real vessel to be anchored here, but otherwise it is an exact fac-simile and has all the fittings that belong to an actual war ship. Officers and crew are detailed by the navy department, and the discipline and mode of life on naval vessels is fully illustrated. Drills are given daily. Located near the battle ship is the Life Saving Station, completely fitted out with living rooms, sleeping rooms and life saving apparatus. Daily exhibitions are also given here for the benefit of visitors. This station will remain permanently in its present location.

MARIAN SHAW.

PALACE OF ARTS

Marian Shaw
Writes of the Stupendous
Manufactures and
Liberal Arts Building.

Its Dimensions Are 787 x 1,687 Feet,
With a Floor Space of 44 Acres.

From Floor to Roof This Structure
Is Crowded With Interesting
Exhibits.

They Are Laid Out in the Form of a
City, Grand, Marvelous and
Unequaled.

CHICAGO, Oct. 5.—[Special Correspondence.]—By far the largest building on the exposition grounds, is that of the manufactures and liberal arts, its dimensions being 787x1687 feet, and having a floor space of 44 acres. It lies along the shore of Lake Michigan, from which it is separated by grassy lawns and promenades. South of it lies the Grand Basin and west the lagoon and North canal. The figures which represent the length and cubic feet of lumber which enter into its construction, the height, length, thickness and sustaining power of its iron arches, beams and braces would be simply bewildering to the unscientific mind, and would convey little idea of its vastness. It is only by comparison that we can approximate its size. It is said that a thousand cottages 25x50 feet could be placed within its walls. A gallery 50 feet wide extends around its four sides, and, projecting from these, are eighty-six smaller galleries. These are approached by thirty great staircases, each 12 feet wide. From floor to roof this vast edifice is filled with exhibits of manufactured articles from almost every nation under the sun. Every branch of manufacture is represented. There are time pieces of every variety, from dainty Geneva watches to the great Polish clock—musical instruments from a simple jewsharp and harmonica to grand pianos and organs—textile fabrics from coarse homespun to the most elegant silks and velvets from the looms of Lyons and Valencia. Rude bead work of the American Indians, delicate hand made laces from Belgium, and exquisite embroideries and tapestries of priceless value mark the various grades of ornamental handiwork. Pottery and ceramic art is illustrated in homely kitchen ware and the most delicate of royal Worcester and Sèvres china. There are tin pans, iron kettles and costly silver vessels inlaid with gold. The work of artists and of artisans finds its exponent here in all varieties of workmanship, and in all degrees of excellence.

The Liberal Arts Building is of the Corinthian style of architecture, relieved by elaborate ornamentation. There are four great entrances designed after the manner of triumphal arches, the central arch of each being forty feet wide and eighty feet high. Besides these main entrances there is at each corner a pavilion forming an arched entrance, similar in design to the great portals. Passing under these arched doorways, we find ourselves in a city, the most unique and cosmopolitan on the globe, representing the people, wares and traffic of every nation of the world. The chief thoroughfare of this wonderful city is Columbia avenue, fifty feet in width and extend-

The Clock Tower in the Liberal Arts and Manufactures Building

"At their intersection stands the great clock tower, which soon becomes a
familiar landmark, and is a favorite rendezvous for weary sight-seers,
and for those who are awaiting friends. 'Meet me at the clock'
is the parting injunction when friends separate to go on
individual tours of discovery."

ing through the center from north to south. Crossing this at the center at right angles is another avenue of equal width. At their intersection stands the great clock tower, which soon becomes a familiar landmark, and is a favorite rendezvous for weary sight-seers, and for those who are awaiting friends. "Meet me at the big clock," is the parting injunction when friends separate to go on individual tours of discovery. This clock tower, rising 120 feet in the exact center of the building, rests upon a base forty feet high. Fronting each of the

four grand avenues are portals twenty-eight feet high and sixteen feet wide, having at each side illustrative historic panels. In the second story of this tower is the office of the director general. Above this are the four faces of the clock, each seven feet in diameter. Within is a chime of bells which marks with melody the passing of every hour. The whole mechanism of the clock, including the chimes, is operated by electricity, the chimes being directly governed by a keyboard similar to that of a piano.

Before setting out on our round of

sight-seeing, let us tarry awhile under the shadow of this great clock and look around us. Along this avenue with its 1,700 feet of length one can see more of the world than anywhere else on earth. Elsewhere you may see broad thoroughfares with their tree-fringed boulevards and luxurious mansions. Euclid avenue, Michigan avenue, Unter den Linden, all have their peculiar charms, but here is a road-way girt by palaces, turrets, domes, pavilions and triumphal monuments. Columbia avenue is the greatest street in the world. When your eyes are wearied with the wealth of ornament which everywhere greets them, turn your attention to the people themselves who are crowding the great artery of this miniature world. Not only do you see passing in procession before you people of all nations, tribes and languages, the fair haired Norse, the dark eyed Southern, yellow Mongolian and swarthy African, but you will see as well every type of American—the pompous capitalist; the rustic farmer; the cultivated man of letters; the shabby clerk trying to make the most of his holiday; the tired, patient, little house-wife who is taking her first outing after years of drudgery; the school-teacher who is doing violence to her conscience by lingering among these beauties when she ought to be upstairs in the educational department studying statistics; bright, radiant college girls, who are intelligently taking in everything, and adding to their already overstocked mental accumulations; the bored dude, and the ennuyed young lady of fashion, who are doing the fair simply because it is the "pwawpah thing," and they can say they've "been there;" people from city, town and country, people of all classes and conditions, young and old, high and low, rich and poor.

If you are rested now we will walk north along this avenue, keeping to the left. Germany's minarets and the great wrought iron gates first attract us. We linger entranced amid the beautiful and artistic exhibits of the royal porcelain works of Berlin—gaze with interest upon costly shields, plates and tankards, gifts of honor to the emperors, to Bismarck and Von Moltke, enter the luxurious and artistic apartments, facsimiles of those of Ludwig, the poor, mad king of Bavaria. In Austria we see more elegant vases and jewels belonging to the imperial collections and albums belonging to the emperor's family.

In the Vienna exhibit are specimens of work turned out in amber, meerschaum, pearl, metal and ivory, exquisite displays of porcelain, majolica, Faience and Bohemian glassware.

The peaked roof and sheltering eaves of Japan's airy castle next invite us. There we find a curious and miscellaneous collection of lacquer and inlaid work, bamboo, raw silks, porcelain in every variety of decoration, and the three great Cloisonne vases, valued at $50,000. One of the most interesting exhibits is the iron eagle, two feet in height and the spread of whose wings from tip to tip measures five feet. The head moves freely like a living bird. There are more than 3,000 feathers, each made separately by hand, and the lines on these feathers number hundreds and even thousands. Five years were consumed in completing this work. Next in order come exhibits of the granite and marble industries of Vermont, mosaics, ceramics, pottery, earthenware, and a fur exhibit, including seventy-five stuffed and mounted animals.

Passing back along the opposite side of Columbia avenue, we take a momentary view of the Gatling guns, Remington, Colt and Winchester fire arms, specimens of Arizona's petrified woods, a huge block of crystal alum weighing eight tons, made from Greenland kryolite, woolen goods, vaults and safes, tools and cutlery, spool silk, gloves, Waterbury watches, Waltham watches, and a thousand other things, too numerous to mention, till we find ourselves again in the vicinity of the great clock and opposite Tiffany's gold and silver palace, resplendent with stained glass, gold and silver plate, diamonds and other precious stones to the value of $500,000. Here is the Magnolia vase valued at $10,000 and the $100,000 diamond. In the Meriden mahogany and plate glass palace we find more gold, silver and jewels to the value of $400,000.

Entering France's magnificent doorways with their elaborately adorned façades, we are lost in a maze of beauty and elegance. We wander from one salon to another, each displaying some peculiar feature of French art and manufac-

The French Exhibit Entrance in the Liberal Arts and Manufactures Building

"Entering France's magnificent doorways with their elaborately adorned façades, we are lost in a maze of beauty and elegance."

ture, exquisite tapestries, delicate china, elegant hangings and upholstery, inlaid furniture, silverware and bronzes—in short, everything in the way of decoration and luxury. Among some of the special exhibits are the Garnier vases, valued at $2,500 each, a cabinet valued at $25,000, the "La France" statue, occupying a position in the center of the French section—a majestic seated fig-

ure, wearing a cuirass, and above whose head in the form of a diadem are the three symbolic figures, "Liberty, Equality, Fraternity." Close to the side of "La France" stands the defiant Gallic cock. The tapestry palace, with its rare Gobelin, Beauvais and Aubusson tapestries, some of which are valued at $100,000, its dainty Sèvres ware, its delicately carved and richly upholstered chairs and divans, inlaid chairs and silken hangings, is a dream of beauty. The display of French dolls arouses ecstasies of delight in the heart of every little girl who beholds them. Doré's bronze vase which from its symbolical design, has been appropriately called "The Poem of the Vine," stands just south of the display of Gobelin tapestries and Sèvres ware. The body of the base is globular, with narrow neck and curved lips. It is 13 feet in height, 7 feet in diameter and rests upon a broad base. Its weight is nearly three tons, and its value, exclusive of duty, $20,000. Adorning its curved sides are hundreds of exquisitely modeled figures, representative of joyous life, while the vine twines gracefully in and out among them. A figure of Bacchus with each arm around a cupid and with one hand holding aloft a cup, ornaments one side, while upon the other a Venus instructs the little love-god in the use of the bow and arrow. Satyrs and bacchantes, birds, bees and butterflies abound—baby faces peer from the vine leaves, and a snake and lizard lie half concealed in the foliage. With all this abundance of detail, so characteristic of its designer, the work yet gives the effect of simplicity.

The zinc palace of Belgium, its bronzes, vases and tapestries next attracts us. True to our feminine instincts, we linger entranced over the exquisite Brussels fans and laces, and leave them with reluctance to gaze at the queer, quaint treasures in the Chinese pagoda. In Russia's magnificent display, which covers over an acre of floor space, we find a repetition of many exhibits already noted. Its display of furs, bronzes and jewels is especially attractive. Norway shows panoramas of mountain scenery, representations of peasants' cottages and costumes, and other characteristic exhibits. In section I, the last on this side of the central avenue, we find a complete and varied collection of musical instruments.

MARIAN SHAW.

40

GENIUS OF AGES.

Exhibits in the Liberal Arts
Building Described by The Argus'
Correspondent.

A "World Within a World,"
Containing All the Products of
Inventive Genius.

CHICAGO, Oct. 8—[Special Correspondence.]—In my last letter I left *The Argus* readers gazing at the large collection of musical instruments in section I, on Columbia avenue in the Manufactures and Liberal Arts Building. Crossing to the opposite side of the avenue, we come upon the beautiful exhibits of Italy and Spain. One thing only is lacking to make the display of these two nations fully equal to any in the whole exposition, and this is space. Their application came late and they have barely half of what they need to show their splendid exhibits to advantage. Besides being crowded, their displays are poorly lighted. But even poor setting and bad lighting cannot entirely obscure the artistic beauty of Italy's exquisite marbles and Spain's relics and art treasures. Aside from the beautiful bronze and marble statuary of Italy there are fine displays of mosaics and inlaid work, filigree and coral jewelry, laces, musical instruments, wood carving, hammered ironwork, damask and silk goods. A fine silver plate about three feet in diameter and valued at $20,000, has pictured upon it in most elaborate chasing a score of mythological tales. Upon an enameled silver coffee pot, whose value is $12,000, are portrayed the leading events of the world's history. The Spanish pavilion is constructed in imitation of the Moorish colonnades in the famous cathedral of Cordova. The largest display comes from Barcelona and includes textile fabrics of satin, silk, cotton, rugs and carpets, mantillas and dainty kerchiefs. From Valencia comes every variety of black silk and marvelous rugs embroidered on cloth of gold. Here also is displayed the ingenious and beautiful work of Felipa Guisasala, vases adorned with solid gold, inlaid and hammered into steel. Wandering through the section devoted to Great Britain we find many things of historic interest, and much which illustrates England's present wealth and greatness. The manufactured exhibits are similar in scope and quality to those displayed by other countries, possessing, perhaps, fewer striking national characteristics. Some of the displays most attractive in their arrangement are Stanforth's exhibit of cutlery, a display of pipes, the pen exhibit of Joseph Gillott, of world wide fame, the "Sunlight Soap" pavilion, the display of Doulton ware, and the Royal Porcelain works. On the top of one pavilion we see a fac-simile in miniature of Windsor castle and grounds. In a case of silverware is a crown worn by H. R. H., the Duke of Essex. In another is a china dessert service used by Queen Victoria. There is also a case of surgical instruments carried by Stanley in his African explorations. The reproduction of the banquet hall of Hatfield house, containing portraits and armor of old-time dignitaries, is interesting to the student of history, and carries us back to the days of "bluff King Hal" and "good Queen Bess."

Hitherto we have attempted to follow out some system in our investigations, but here in this wonderful palace of mechanic arts, with its embarrassment of riches, we grow reckless, over-

The American Bronze Company Exhibit in the Liberal Arts and Manufacures Building

"There is * * * [following a listing of many things, including this gigantic
bronze statue of Columbus] * * * in short everything which the genius
of man has devised for the use and comfort of the human race, to
supply their wants, to gratify their whims and fancies."

whelmed as nowhere else by vastness and comprehensiveness. In despair we lay aside notebook and pencil, and with a feeling of littleness and helplessness, "do naught but gaze and gaze," with ever increasing wonder and delight. We no longer attempt to "do" the sections in the order laid down in the guide-books; we throw statistics to the winds, and seeking only for entertainment, wander aimlessly in and out amid the mazes of this labyrinth. Surprises await us at every turn. Here is an engine with tender and coach made of spool silk, here a suspension bridge constructed of Kirk's soap. Now our eyes are dazzled by the sparkling cut-glass exhibit of the Libbey Glass company. Now we walk

past rows upon rows of stoves and ranges. Here we see nothing but clocks; in another place, cases upon cases of toilet articles and perfumery. In Switzerland we find rare and beautiful wood-carvings,—in Brazil, dazzling collections of mosaics, gems and precious stones. In Canada is an Indian school at work, presided over by sweet-faced sisters of charity. In East India are ornate carvings, and inlaid work, and ancient Hindoo idols. In Ceylon we are entertained by jugglery, and native curiosities. Here is the Waterbury Watch company's "Century" clock, which cost $80,000 and was ten years in the process of construction, every part being carved by hand. Here is a representation of Greeley's expedition to the north pole—here the Monaco vase, owned by the pope. It was four years in making and there is only one other like it in the world. There is the wonderful toy exhibit of Vienna, majestic fire places and porcelain ranges from Hamburg, a wax portrait of Pocahontas, a gigantic bronze statue of Columbus, a wonderful and unique display of varnishes and guns, a pavilion of fireworks, a bridal veil worth $7,000, corsets of silk and satin trimmed with gold and silver lace, and clasped by big diamond butterflies—in short everything which the genius of man has devised for the use and comfort of the human race, to supply their wants, to gratify their whims and fancies. Were there time, we might speak at length of the architectural beauties of the various pavilions, in each of which one sees something characteristic of the nation which it represents. The styles of architecture within this immense temple of liberal arts are as varied as those found upon the grounds outside. Everywhere one meets with groups of statuary, historical, fanciful and mythological, beautiful in workmanship, and appropriate in design.

The galleries of this building are chiefly devoted to exhibits of various educational institutions. Colleges, universities, public and private schools from nearly every state in the union and from many foreign nations are represented. To the educator and the scientist a vast field of research and investigation is here opened. Aside from institutions of learning, there are also exhibits of various religious bodies, of societies humanitarian and reformatory. The journalistic world has also a fine representation.

The visitor who has plenty of time at his command, will return to this "world within a world" again and again, and at each new coming will see something to interest, charm and instruct.

MARIAN SHAW.

CAGED LIGHTNING

Marian Shaw Writes of the
Electricity Building at the
World's Fair.

Marvelous Exhibit of the Most
Wonderful Force Controlled
by Man.

Thousands of Ways in Which It Is
Made to Labor for Its Master.

Wonders of the Inner World
Revealed in the Mines and
Mining Building.

CHICAGO, Oct. 13.—[Special Correspondence]—Between the southern end of the lagoon and the Administration Building, facing the Court of Honor, stands the Palace of Electricity. As in many other of the exposition buildings, so in this we find a union of different kinds of architecture, the Doric and Corinthian prevailing, but relieved by much ornate decoration. At each of the four corners is a pavilion surmounted by a light open spire 169 feet high. On the east and west sides between these pavilions and the center pavilion is another, bearing a low, square dome upon an open lantern. An open portico extends along the whole length of the south façade. The pitched roof of the nave and transept and the flat roof of the main part of the building are lighted by many sky-lights, and the pavilions are furnished with a multitude of windows and balconies. The exterior deco-ration is elaborate and rich, illustrating by various figures in relief upon the panels, friezes and spandrels, the purpose of the building. The general effect is of marble, enriched in its porticos and loggia by color and bronze effects. In front of the entrance stands a bronze statue of Benjamin Franklin with his kite. Above the main portal one reads the legend, *"Caelo fulmen rapuit."* Over the other entrances appear the names of celebrated electricians, although none now living have been thus honored. There are in this structure 40,000 panes of glass which sparkle at night with a splendor beyond the power of pen to describe. The exhibits within the building include all the appliances of electricity, and the latest inventions and improvements in electrical machinery, of which there is a bewildering variety scarcely credible to the uninitiated. The workings of this wonderful force are shown in electric motors, elevators, machinery of all kinds—in metallurgy, chemistry, electroplating, gilding, forging, welding—in telephones, audiophones, signal apparatus, phonographs, telautographs—in photography, cooking, dentistry, therapeutics—as a remedial agent in preserving life, and as an instrument of capital punishment in destroying it—in a thousand other ways which, to the unscientific mind, seem little short of miracle or witchcraft. Not only is an overwhelming multitude of displays made within the building, but the uses of electricity may be seen in the illumination of the grounds and in the great electric motor at the power house, which distributes light and power to all the other buildings. There is also the Intramural railway which has been denominated the biggest thing in electricity at the fair, and is thought to have solved the problem of the application of electricity to elevated roads. Not only are all the commercial and economic uses of electricity illustrated here, but one may trace the whole history—brief but glorious—of the discovery and development of this mighty force. Its existence as a science is measured by decades rather than by centuries, but what can the centuries show in other lines of research and invention as marvelous as even one decade in this? So rapid and so widely spread has been its advance that the mere schoolboy now talks learnedly of a force of which, fifty years ago, the wisest sage was ignorant. In contemplation of the wonderful advance in this direction we call to mind a few lines of a poem, "The Song of the Lightning," written subsequent to the invention of the telegraph, in which this haughty boast is made:

"Away! away! through the sightless air,
    Stretch forth your iron thread!
For I would not dim my sandals fair,
    With the dust ye tamely tread!

Though I cannot toil, like the groaning slave
    Ye have fettered with iron skill
To ferry you over the boundless wave,
    Or grind in the noisy mill!

No! No! I'm the spirit of light and love,
    To my unseen hand 'tis given,
To pencil the ambient clouds above
    And polish the stars of heaven."

Science now laughs to score this vain challenge. It has captured and fettered this most illusive and intangible of elements, and has made it a servant of servants. It is true that like a blind and captive Samson, it sometimes rises in its strength and revenges itself upon its captor, but the close of this century will doubtless see it wholly subdued and obedient to every wish of its master. It is given only to the learned and scientific thoroughly to appreciate the wonders of the electrical display, but the ordinary observer may experience enjoyment and delight from the useful results and beautiful effects which his wiser brethren have brought into existence through its wondrous agency. It is not necessary that one should be learned or scientific in order to enjoy the beautiful spectacle presented by the exposition grounds at night, which lighted up by 8,000 arc and 130,000 incandescent lamps, when the jets of the electric fountains are rising and falling with ever changing iridescent light—when the great search light, whose surface intensity is 194,000,000 candle power, throws its far reaching beams to the remotest corner of the grounds, now lighting up the golden dome of the Administration Building, and now the exquisite groups of statuary, which adorn the Peristyle and the marble like buildings that surround the Court of Honor; which now reveals the majestic proportions of the gilded statue of the republic, now rests upon that beautiful creation of MacMonnies, the Columbian fountain, and now lingers for a moment upon the graceful Diana, poised in mid air upon the summit of the Agricultural Building; when the Grand Basin, with gondolas and electric launches flitting hither and thither upon its blue waters, mirrors back from its surface the thousand sparkling lights that glitter under the eaves of the palaces which girt its shores. The glorious beauty of this sight strikes the beholder dumb. The words of the apocalypse come involuntarily into his mind: "And I saw the holy city, New Jerusalem, coming down from God out of heaven, prepared as a bride adorned for her husband-having the glory of God, and her light was like unto a stone most precious, even like a jasper stone, clear as crystal."

Whatever faults the over-zealous critic may find in the details of architecture or ornamentation, however much he may cavil at the inartistic effects produced by crude coloring and sculpture, his must indeed be an insensible and brutal mind, who can fail to be affected

Gondolas in the Basin, in front of the MacMonnies Fountain

"* * * when the great search light, whose surface intensity is
194,000,000 candle power, throws its far reaching beams
to the remotest corner of the grounds * * * [and] now
rests upon that beautiful creation of MacMonnies,
the Columbian fountain."

by the loveliness of this transcendently lovely sight.

A few steps across a narrow avenue brings us to the Palace of Mines and Mining. This building faces the lagoon on the north and the Grand plaza on the south. It is constructed after the early Italian renaissance with a mingling of French design in the interior. Over the main doorway is a classical, allegorical figure representing the industry to which the building is devoted. A colossal, half-reclining female figure in Greek draperies holds aloft in one hand a lamp to guide the miner, in the other a pick. There is very little of exterior mural decoration, and the interior is also plain but appropriate. In no other building is there a greater diversity of exhibits. There include not only the grosser and commoner useful metals, building stones, soils, salts, petroleum, etc., but the precious metals, together with a dazzling display of diamonds, opals and gems of every description. In these exhibits every state in the union, and almost every nation on earth is represented. A successful effort has been made to render the exhibits of each attractive. North Carolina has a mica pavilion, Kentucky a representation of a section of Mammoth cave, Iowa a miniature coal mine, New Mexico a miner's cabin built of the various mineral products of the state. Many other state pavilions are built entirely of native products. Notable among these are Colorado, Wisconsin, Missouri, Indiana and Ohio. The pavilions of many foreign governments are remarkable for their gorgeous effects. Chief among these are France, Germany and New South Wales. Besides native ores and minerals, there are also shown many working models of mining machinery, various processes of reducing metals, together with relief maps of different mining sections, photographs of scenery in the mining districts, and various pamphlets setting forth their mineral resources and the development of mining industries. There is a laboratory and a library of 5,000 volumes on mining and metallurgy, said to be the most complete of its kind in existence. It is impossible, in the limited space of a newspaper article, to mention one one-hundredth part of the attractive exhibits. The "Silver Queen," from Aspen, Colorado, is one of the most popular features. This represents the seventeen year old state of Colorado under the guise of a graceful maiden seated in a silver barge mounted on wheels, having above her head a canopy of glittering crystals. The figure is of heroic size, and the whole rests upon a pedestal covered with gold, silver and other minerals. Gold and silver figures of Plutus, the god of riches, bearing cornucopias from which flow streams of the precious metal, complete the group. The silver statue of Justice in the Montana section attracts universal attention. The famous actress, Ada Rehan, posed as the model for this fine work of art. Prominent among other displays rises the great iron and steel tower of Baron Stumm in the German section. Michigan has a unique display illustrative of her copper industry. In New South Wales, raised upon a lofty column, is a heroic and beautiful statue of Atlas bearing the world upon his shoulders. Denmark has a model in silver of a viking ship. Arizona and New Mexico have brilliant and sparkling exhibits of ores. There is a mass of almost pure copper weighing 6,200 pounds, miles of drawn wire and sheets of copper bright as a polished mirror. A pyramid of zinc and lead marks the location of Missouri; a great shaft of coal that of Pennsylvania. A block of coal from Washington measures twenty-four feet, eight inches in width and four feet, eight inches in height, and weighs nearly twenty-two

Colorado Exhibit in the Mines and Mining Building

"The 'Silver Queen' from Aspen, Colorado, is one of the most popular features. This represents the seventeen year old state of Colorado under the guise of a graceful maiden seated in a silver barge mounted on wheels, having above her head a canopy of glittering crystals."

tons. There is a diamond exhibit from South Africa guarded by native Zulus. The exhibit of Greece is chiefly archeological, showing many relics and ancient methods of mining. There are tools and utensils older than Athens. Some articles of apparel and household utensils are shown which were found in shafts left by the ancients. Much of the mining of today is carried on in these same old shafts. Indeed the illustrations of modern methods of mining in this classic land show very little advance over the methods employed ages ago. The chief interest of this display attaches to its historic character. A beautiful specimen of marble from the island of Skyros is shown which is said to be equal for purposes of sculpture to the far-famed Parian.

A unique statue of liberty in salt, facetiously called "Lot's Wife," comes from the famous Avery salt mines of Louisiana. Rare specimens of orange-red crystal, bright crystals of azurite, with velvet tufts of malachite come from the Pacific coast. There are deep red garnets from Alaska, a precious turquoise from Los Cerrilez, New Mexico. From the south Atlantic coast region come amethysts, sapphires and aqua marines, and from every part of the world gems whose luster dazzles the eye, but whose unpronounceable, scientific names would only bewilder the reader. We leave the mining building more than ever impressed with the wonderful wealth and resources of Old Mother Earth. We have looked upon and admired the useful, rare and beautiful products of her teeming soil, bowed in awe and reverence before the mysterious, hidden forces that hover unseen above and around her, and now we marvel at the untold wealth and beauty that has for ages lain concealed within her bosom. Not only the "deep unfathomed caves of ocean," but desert wastes, rock-ribbed hills and measureless caverns hide "full many a gem of purest ray serene."

MARIAN SHAW.

MODES OF TRAVEL

Progress of Transportation as
Illustrated at the World's Fair.

Evolution of Railroad Conveyance
Shown in Its Successive Stages.

"John Bull" Engine of 1830
Contrasted with Locomotives
of Today.

All Other Known Methods of
Transportation Placed on
Exhibition.

CHICAGO, Oct. 16—[Special Correspondence.]—Standing upon the avenue which runs north of the mining building, and looking toward the west, the magnificent portal of the Transportation Building, called the "Golden Door," meets our view. This grand doorway consists of a series of receding arches covered with gold leaf, the exterior arch being adorned with allegorical figures and groups in bas-relief. On one side is a panel showing an ancient ox cart to illustrate primitive modes of travel. On the other modern means of transportation are shown by a railway train with all its elegant accessories. To the left of this golden archway is inscribed the following aphorism from Lord Bacon: "There be three things which make a nation great and prosperous—a fertile soil, busy workshops, and easy conveyance for men and animals from place to place." On the right are these words of Macaulay: "Of all inventions, the alphabet and printing press alone excepted, those inventions which abridge distance have done the most for mankind." The remainder of the building, aside from this ornate and splendid entrance, has been variously commented upon by critics. Where connoisseurs are so at variance, one unenlightened in the details of art and architecture will scarcely venture to give an opinion. It is admitted by most that, as regards architecture and design, this building is simple, dignified and harmonious, but the coloring, the striking and original ornamentation shocks the delicate sense of the would be critic, and "makes him to shudder and grow sick at heart." In striking contrast with the other great buildings of the exposition, this is a bright terra cotta color, with elaborate frescoes and grotesque ornamentation. Between the windows, on a waving background of pink and green, are angels of heroic size with outstretched wings and holding a scroll in their extended hands. The wings are supposed to symbolize rapidity of movement, but what else is typified by this somewhat prim, modestly gowned, bare-footed female figure, no one but the designer can guess. Besides these there is a maze of friezes, disks and panels of which no one seems to know the meaning or motive. This exterior is characterized by some as hideous and irritating, while other declare it to be unique and interesting, and a pleasant relief from the dazzling whiteness of the remaining buildings. But however tastes may differ in respect to the outside, there is but one verdict regarding the contents of these highly ornamented walls. They form one of the most interesting and instructive exhibits of the exposition. Every method of transportation is here displayed, from the primitive bull-cart of the East Indian, to the most elaborate and elegant of modern carriages. We see here the first awkward and ill-constructed locomotive that dragged its old-fashioned coach at a snail's pace over the first American railway, and the splendid, awe-inspiring iron monster that, with its long, heavily-loaded trains, flies with the speed of a hurricane over the smooth, shining steel rails of our modern railways. Added to these are marine methods of transportation of every kind, vehicles for common roads, bicycles, pneumatic machines, balloons and flying machines. Eight acres are devoted to railway exhibits. On one side of the chief aisle in this department we see long rows of primitive locomotives, each succeeding one showing some new invention or appliance constituting an improvement over its predecessor. Notable among these early pioneers is the "John Bull," the first locomotive ever run in America. Once a marvel of mechanism, it is now a relic of the past, and, in comparison with its magnificent descendants, "a thing to be laughed at." It was built by George Stevenson in England in 1830, to run on the Camden & Amboy railroad. This locomotive, then the wonder of the age, weighed ten tons. Its four drive wheels were made of wood with cast-iron hubs and iron tires. The capacity of the boiler was 1,500 gallons. When this wonderful machine arrived in Philadelphia, but one man was found among the puzzled mechanics who had skill enough to put it together. This at last being successfully accomplished, it made its trial trip, carrying a head of thirty pounds of steam pressure. The engine which we see here displays its greatest degree of perfection after five years experiment and improvement. The wooden pilot and the cow-catcher were among those improvements. There are also the "Atlantic," 1832, the first American engine in existence; the "Best Friend," the first built for actual service

in America; "the Jefferson," 1835; the "Mazeppa," 1886; the "Sandusky," 1837, the first used west of the Ohio river. The first locomotive ever to enter Chicago was the "Pioneer," built in 1836. Its original cost was $3,500. After running twelve years on the Utica & Schenectady road and twenty-six on the Chicago & Galena line, it was honorably mustered out of service. The first American railway coach, resembling an old fashioned stage coach, is also on exhibition. It has comfortable seating capacity for four persons. There is little provision for ventilation, none for toilet purposes, and tallow dips at night serve only to make the darkness more intense. Such were the discomforts of travel to which our immediate ancestors were subjected, and yet they thought it luxury. In 1840 the happy thought of some humanitarian materialized in the introduction into this coach of a tank of drinking water. Leading up by easy stages from these old time engines and coaches we reach the acme of modern elegance and comfort in the Pullman palace and vestibuled trains. The self-indulgent and luxurious millionaire, traveling in one of these, misses nothing which his own palatial home can furnish him. These trains need no description, for even the humblest traveller of today is familiar with all their magnificent details. The American railway section outranks in perfection and finish the display of all other nations. The English engines are clumsy looking affairs and the English palace cars, too grand and expensive for the average Englishman, are ugly and ill-arranged in comparison with our own. A French railway coach is also displayed which resembles an ordinary American omnibus. In connection with the railway exhibit are hundreds of devices essential to rapid and safe railway travel—air brakes, buffers, couplers, etc.—all American inventions.

But if America can boast of her superiority as regards her railways, she must yield the palm to foreign nations when it comes to a comparison of marine methods of transportation. Every vessel of size or note in the naval or merchant marine service of Great Britain is represented here by a model or by designs and drawings. An immense chart with hundreds of tiny models clinging to its surface will show you the whereabouts of every great Atlantic, Pacific or Southern Pacific vessel, its location and the latest tidings from it, with the hour when last heard from. You will be convinced, after a few hours' study of England's naval and marine resources, that "Britannia" does indeed "rule the wave." Here one looks with melancholy interest upon the splendid model of the ill-fated Victoria, which, only a short time ago, sank beneath the blue waters of the Mediterranean, carrying with her 400 of England's brave seamen. The flag at half-mast and the black bunting which flies in place of the pennant commemorate this sad event. There are also exhibited fine models of French steamships, together with a panoramic display, showing elegant interiors and equipments. Although America can not rank first in her marine display, yet in the beautiful model of a Red Star line steamship she shows herself no mean rival of her sisters across the sea. A huge section of a vessel, showing a portion of each deck, gives a clear idea of the accommodations to be found on a first-class ocean steamer. Smaller crafts of every description are displayed from the cajak and birchbark canoe of the Esquimau and North American Indian to the silk and rubber canoes and steam and electric launches of today. There are dug-outs from Africa, a fisherman's boat from the sea of Galilee, old Norse Viking ships, the boat in which Grace Darling performed her noble and wonderful deed of rescue, a native Brazilian canoe fifty feet long and models of Spanish men-of-war of the latest type. In connection with the marine display are also numberless models of bridges and canals.

The bicycle exhibit is extensive and interesting, showing the evolution of the bicycle from the awkward "dandy-horse" used by the Earl of Durham in 1810, to the graceful "Safety" and "Columbia" of the present day, including tandems, triplets and every existing variety of this ingenious and useful machine. Wheeled vehicles of every description are shown. Ancient sedan-chairs, palanquins, old-fashioned stage and mail-coaches stand side by side with the most elaborate and elegant carriages of all sorts, styles and names. In the exhibit from Siam are found bullock carriages, joss-chairs used by priests in carrying idols, blue chairs for weddings and green chairs for officials. Among the relics is a wagon 150 years old, belonging to Nancy Standish Welles of Connecticut, a descendant of Miles Standish. There are curious sleds from Madeira, constructed not for swift travel over snow and ice, but over smoothly paved and slippery streets. From this country also come the curious mountain sleds, so constructed as to slide down the well-worn mountain paths with incredible speed, moving, it is said, at a rate of from thirty to thirty-five miles an hour. There is a sled of spruce from Unalakit, with the runners made from the jaw-bone of a whale, a Yukon river sled, hunting sleds, toboggans, skates and snow shoes.

In this building are represented the origin, growth and development of the various methods and transportation used among all natives and in all ages. The historical feature is kept clearly in view, and even the most careless observer will leave this building wiser, as regards his knowledge of transportation, than when he entered it. In addition to the great object lesson presented by the exhibits there are numerous photographs, drawings, books, pamphlets and reports bearing upon the subject.

MARIAN SHAW.

THE PERFUMED PALACE.

What World's Fair Visitors Find in the Beautiful Horticultural Hall.

CHICAGO, Oct. 18—[Special Correspondence.]—Just north of the Transportation Building lies the Palace of Horticulture, where the lover of the beautiful in nature may spend hours "treading out fragrance, drinking perfume." The building is the finest ever erected for the purpose, and has connected with it numerous lawns, courts and conservatories, altogether covering over six acres of ground. It is impossible to do more than simply mention some of the most effective exhibits, which include flowers, plants and fruits of every description, the products of every zone. In the month of May the indoor display included roses, orchids, carnations and rhododendrons; out of doors were tulips, pansies and hyacinths in full bloom. Then came azaleas, and in June the flowering annuals and perennials displayed a wealth of beauty and fragrance. Each month has had its special glory. August and September brought myriad varieties of hollyhocks, asters and clematis, to be followed in turn by October, with its special floral offerings. A magnificent display of

San Bernardino County Exhibit of Oranges and Lemons in the Horticultural Hall

"It is impossible to do more than simply mention some of the most effective exhibits, which include flowers, plants and fruits of every description, the products of every zone."

chrysanthemums will crown this flower festival. Time would fail to speak of the varieties of tropical and aquatic plants, of the rare shrubs, bamboos, cacti, palms and ferns from every corner of the globe. The century plant and night-blooming cereus add their beauty and fragrance to the wealth of splendor and perfume that everywhere greets our senses. Not only "all the perfumes of Araby" but the concentrated sweetness of all the flowers on earth seem to mingle under the crystal dome of the floral palace. The display extends outside of the building, including Wooded Island, and large spaces adjoining other buildings. In several pavilions are exhibits of the vintages of various wine producing countries, this exhibition being in some cases enhanced by panoramic views, fountains of wine and rustic grottos. The orange tower, the miniature mountain, seventy-five feet high, upon which are giant tree-ferns, palms and many other rare plants; the crystal cavern beneath it; a representation of the national capitol in white immortelles, and the roof garden are notable among other beautiful displays.

MARIAN SHAW.

ON THE MIDWAY

Sights That Greet the Eye of the
Visitor to This Play-Ground
of Nations,

Where Savage and Barbarian Mingle
with Their More Enlightened
Fellows.

An Interesting Picture of Home Life
in Every Country of the Globe.

Wonders of the Orient and Occident
Displayed in One Vast Group.

CHICAGO, Oct. 25—[Special Correspondence.]—We have done so much sober sight-seeing in the past few days, have taken in so much of the serious and dignified element of the fair, that we begin to feel the need of a little relaxation and amusement, and where can this be found, if not on the Midway plaisance, that summer play-ground of nations where all the serious business of life seems to be laid aside, and all peoples, tongues, nations and languages have assembled for a summer holiday. Much has been said and written of the Midway plaisance as affording a grand opportunity for ethnological study, and as being an equivalent for foreign travel—a place where one can study the peculiarities and customs of the various nations represented, as if under their own vine and fig tree. On the other hand, much has been said of the immoralities and vulgarities of this unique pleasure-ground. One should not make the mistake of adopting either extreme of opinion. The people of the Midway are typical only to a certain extent. They represent some phases of foreign life, but it is life in its most whimsical aspect, and it would be as unfair to take them as representatives of their respective nations as to take Buffalo Bill's "Wild West" show as typical of American life. The phases of life seen in the plaisance are both interesting and amusing. As for the vulgarities, unfortunately they exist, but no one is compelled to look upon them. Although the nations of the earth are not seen here in their highest degree of culture, one meets with a civilization so strange and bizarre that he seems as if transported, now to medieval times, now to a period still more remote. These people are they, who, in the mad race of nations for power and pelf, seem to have been left far behind, and, compared with the nations of today, are like untutored children. From the Bedouins of the desert and the South Sea Islanders, one can here trace, from living models, the progress of the human race from savagery and barbarism through all the intermediate stages to a condition still many degrees removed from the advanced civilization of the nineteenth century. As great a diversity of religions exist as degrees of enlightenment. Here are devotees appeasing their deity by weird dances and self-inflicted tortures, here the muezzin calls the devout Moslem to prayer, the Chinaman bows before his gods in the Joss house and the pious Catholic crosses himself before the image of the Virgin.

The strip of land which holds this heterogeneous collection of races is 600 feet broad and contains eighty acres. It was formerly a popular shaded driveway connecting Jackson and Washington parks. Now it is the temporary and peaceful abode of people who, a few centuries ago, had they chanced to meet, would have challenged each other to mortal combat. Let us make a tour of this motley world. Walking down the cosmopolitan avenue, jostled by men of every race, color and creed, with quaint faces and quainter costumes, we are first attracted by the shrill squeak of a bagpipe. Upon investigation we find that these weird strains proceed from the picturesque walls of Donegal castle. The merry piper, who, with his white hair and true Celtic cast of countenance, is no less picturesque than his surroundings, is McSweeney. All day long he pipes as blithely as if he were standing upon his native sod. Here is one of two Irish villages which are under the respective supervision of Lady Aberdeen and Mrs. Ernest Hart, two philanthropic ladies, who have done much for the Irish working-classes. These villages consist of typical Irish cottages, thatched with turf brought from the Emerald isle, pieces of which Erin's emigrant sons are permitted to carry away as souvenirs of the fair, and pleasant reminders of their native land. In these villages are carried on many of the industries common to the Irish peasantry. The girls under the immediate charge of Lady Aberdeen are employed in hand-weaving, spinning, knitting, lace-making, embroidery, butter-making and all kinds of dairy-work. An elaborate display is made of Irish metal work, and here are found reproductions of many relics whose history in some cases covers a period of more than a thousand years. In this collection is to be found the "Bell of St. Patrick," the history of which can be traced back through 1,400 years. Then there is the Tara brooch, one of the earliest specimens of Irish art ever discovered. It is a composite of copper and tin called white bronze. Upon its face are traced designs found in early illuminated manuscripts. The delicate tracery of the inlaid work cannot be seen except through a powerful lens. There is also the Kilkenny brooch, made of white metal, and dating from 1050. And then there is the shrine containing St. Patrick's tooth, which that worthy is supposed to have dropped on the doorsill of old St. Bron's church in Killaspugbrone. The originals of these relics are in the museum of the Royal Irish academy, and are never allowed to leave that depository. Let us climb the towers of Blarney castle, and get one of the finest views to be had on the exposition grounds. Do not forget before descending to press your lips to the famous kissing-stone, and thereby acquire that eloquence and fluency of speech for which Erin's sons and daughters are famous.

The Javanese village next claims our attention. It consists of a picturesque collection of twenty bamboo houses, set in the midst of tropical palm trees. These buildings, apparently flimsy, are in reality very strong, impervious to rain, and yet so light as to be unaffected by earthquakes. They are built on stilts to insure protection from snakes, which infest the native soil of these people. Here are shown various phases of Java's domestic life and employments. The strange and varying notes of the gong-orchestra invite the visitor to enter the theater, where he will be entertained with jugglery, dancing, fencing, wrestling and snake-charming. The "wajang-wong" or Javanese dance consists of a succession of graceful poses, forming a pantomine, which is part of a continuous story.

The German village, our next objective point, contains an old feudal castle of the fifteenth century, with moat, drawbridge and palisades, and a group of typical peasant houses. On the village common is represented a rural fair, where, in booths, various articles of manufacture are offered for sale. Within the castle is a museum comprising a famous collection of weapons. There are here many historic features of an ideal German village,—the ancient town hall, the market place and the inevitable saloon, the latter being in the style of 1570.

In the street of "Old Cairo" may be seen a perfect representation of the narrow roadway, and picturesque architecture of the old Egyptian city, with its balconied houses and curious ornamentation of open wood-work. Here are also an ancient mosque, and a temple resembling closely that of Luxor, built 1,550 B.C., with monoliths, obelisks, colossal statues, sphinxes and hieroglyphic inscriptions. Many curiosities and antiquities are offered for sale in the bazaar. In this street may be witnessed the curious ceremonies of an Egyptian wedding and a birthday festival. Patient camels with their drivers are in attendance, and those desiring it may ride through the quaint street perched aloft upon one of these "ships of the desert," or, if they prefer, they may be jolted over the rough pavements on the backs of diminutive donkeys, driven by barefooted, yelling little Arabs, who, clad in long, dirty white garments resembling night gowns, scream and hoot and pummel the long-suffering little beasts with their sticks. Young America has long been noted for his marvelous lung power, but the little howling Cairo-street Arab can far surpass him in vocal gymnastics, both as regards variety and

Old Cairo Scene in the Midway Plaisance

"In the street of 'Old Cairo' may be seen a perfect representation of the narrow roadway, and picturesque architecture of the old Egyptian city, with its balconied houses and curious ornamentation of open wood-work."

intensity of the shrill sounds that issue from his barbarous little throat. The chief of the camel drivers, himself a curiosity, is Achmet, an Egyptian guide and well known to foreign travelers. Cairo, too, has its theatre, but as its exhibitions are not of a nature to suit refined tastes, we forbear to enter. Hideous dances and exhibitions of jugglery are carried on at almost every corner, accompanied by ear-torturing music. We are not sorry to leave Old Cairo, nor do we care to tarry long among the natives of Algeria, where may be seen the shocking brutalities of the torture dance, performed to the deafening clang of cymbals.

In the Chinese opera house almond-eyed Celestials will entertain you with a play, abridged, to suit occidental tastes, from four months in execution to the limit of an hour—and you will find this quite long enough. In these plays the staple characters are emperors, princesses and Joss, the high god. The female parts are taken by men. There are no stage illusions and changes of scenery and all stage business are carried on in full sight of the audience. The hoarse clangor of Chinese gongs accompanies the performance.

American Indians, artistically painted in chrome yellow, vermillion and green, with feathers, knives, tomahawks and all the horrid accoutrements of savage warfare, perform their war dance for the delectation of visitors, keeping time to their orchestra, which thumps out a maddening and interminable tune consisting of one note. Their saltatory efforts are a little less dreadful than the frenzied torture dance of the Algerians, but still sufficiently harrowing.

We turn to scenes more pastoral and peaceful and enter the ostrich farm. After amusing ourselves a while with watching these queer feathered bipeds, we start on our return trip, taking in the attractions on the other side of the avenue. We remain only a short time in the Lapland and Dahomey villages, the former with its population of twenty-four human beings, twelve reindeer and five dogs, the latter numbering sixty-nine persons, including twenty-one Amazonian warriors. The music is quite as nerve-torturing as any we have heard, and the fetish Amazonian war dance leaves us little choice between this and the other barbarous so-called dances. In the Austrian village and in "Old Vienna" we seem to have returned again to civilization, albeit of a somewhat ancient type. Here in this street, made to represent a street of the Austrian capital as it existed 150 years ago, we see a quaint, but refined and ideal life. In the shops are carried on many industries, some of them of a highly artistic character, including amber, meerschaum and ivory-turning, carving, modeling, embroidering, lace manufacture, and many other processes. The "Rath-haus," church, and dwelling houses are in the style of the seventeenth century. The service in the shops and café is by men and women in Austrian costumes. Our ears, worn out by the frightful clang and jangle of oriental music, are here rested and charmed by the sweet notes and divine harmonies of the Austrian band.

We pause a few moments to gaze at the beautiful model of St. Peter's church, one-sixteenth the dimensions of the original, but a perfect reproduction even to the minutest details. Now we find ourselves in the shadow of the wonderful Ferris wheel, from the top of which, 260 feet above terra-firma, we may view the counterfeit presentment of "all the kingdoms of the world and the glory of them." Literally, we can see from this lofty look-out the whole of Jackson park, Chicago with its suburbs, miles and miles of the blue expanse of

Lake Michigan, the states of Wisconsin, Michigan and Indiana, and far into the interior of Illinois. This wonderful piece of mechanism, a description of which is unnecessary, as it is so familiar to all, takes the place of the Eiffel tower, which was the wonder of the Paris exposition. A model of this tower is shown here.

In the Moorish palace, built after the style of the famous Alhambra of Granada, is a theater of optical illusions. Here, by the ingenious arrangement of numerous mirrors, charming gardens and luxurious apartments are made to stretch out into limitless space, their beauties and exquisite ornamentations being multiplied and reproduced by these magic mirrors. It is a veritable fairyland or Aladdin's palace of wonders. Columns adorned with carvings and hieroglyphics, arched ceilings studded with gems and mother-of-pearl, reflect subdued light. Filigree work in gold, purple and silver adorns the archways. Concealed pictures, reflected by the ubiquitous mirror, give the illusion of beautiful scenery—long stretches of beach, mountains, ravines, and leaping cataracts. Here too is seen that wonderful young woman, Magenta, who floats through the air on nothing, Galatea, who blushes into life one moment, then fades to pale marble, and next changes to a basket of roses. A lotus flower, floating on the bosom of the water, blossoms into a beautiful woman's head. Mystified by these marvels of magic, we leave this land of enchantment and are transported to scenes far more real and substantial, if less agreeable.

In the Turkish village there is more oriental dancing, with its sinuous, languorous grace, weddings, funerals and merry-makings, while every type of musical instrument strives to outdo the others, and all unite in making a hideous din. The Bedouin camp nearby shows all the features of life in the desert. A Persian tent 400 years old, embroidered in gold and silver, and Cleopatra's needles are among the curiosities. The South Sea Islanders present us with more features of semi-barbarism, and split our ears with more frightful music. We are glad to leave this human exhibit for awhile, and find entertainment in watching the marvelous tricks and performanes of Hagenbeck's trained animals. A visit to the Libbey and Venetian glass works completes our experiences on the plaisance. We leave behind us without regret this fantastical conglomeration of strange people, with their antipodal customs, dress and amusements.

MARIAN SHAW.

WORK OF WOMAN

Her Progress During the Past
Century Illustrated at the
Columbian Exposition.

Woman's Building a Fitting
Monument to the Emancipation
of Her Sex.

In Art, Science and Literature Do
the Fair Ones of This Earth Excel.

A Glimpse Into the Building
Where Tiny Rulers of the
Land Are Cared For.

CHICAGO, Oct. 27.—[Special Correspondence.]—Stepping back into the nineteenth century from what seems a confused dream of the past, we see before us the graceful and classic outlines of the Woman's building, that monument of the best the world has to show of human progress, since it signalizes the emancipation of woman, who from her ancient condition of disgraceful servitude, has risen to be the equal and co-laborer of her former master. The Woman's palace fronts the lagoon which here expands into a bay about 400 feet wide. It stands on an elevation ten feet above the water, from which it is separated by grounds adorned with shrubs and flowers. This building, constructed after the style of the Italian renaissance is itself an exponent of woman's skill, being designed by Miss Sophia G. Hayden, to whom also was awarded its execution. The display within the building duplicates to a great extent that found in other buildings, with this difference—everything here represents the work of woman. Woman's achievements in every branch of industry is found within these walls. Women of every nation on the earth have contributed to these exhibits, which are interesting not only from their beauty of design, skillful workmanship and intrinsic value, but especially interesting as showing the rapid advancement made by woman during the past hundred years. They form an object lesson in the history of woman's intellectual development, and present an unanswerable argument to those who have been wont to deny her ability to excel in any line of work outside that of light fancy work or household drudgery. Not only in all departments of art, science and literature, has woman entered into competition with man, but the work of woman artisans, as illustrated here, shows that she can successfully compete with him even in those industries which demand the exercise of muscular power. This is well illustrated by the display of iron work wrought upon the anvil by a young lady of California, and also by the exhibit of an English woman blacksmith. The mention of most of the exhibits here would only be a repetition of much that has already been described, so we will content ourselves with pointing out a few of the most attractive and interesting.

Walking along the gallery on the second floor our attention is drawn to a long, narrow piece of tapestry, extending the whole length of the wall on one side. The crudeness of execution and the quaint figures indicate its antiquity. This is a fac-simile of the famous Bayeux tapestry wrought by Matilda of Flanders to celebrate the victory of her royal husband, William the Conqueror, over the Saxons in 1066. The busy nee-

The Woman's Building

"* * * we see before us the graceful and classic outlines of the Woman's building, that monument of the best the world has to show of human progress, since it signalizes the emancipation of woman, who from her ancient condition of disgraceful servitude, has risen to be the equal and co-laborer of her former master."

dle and superhuman patience of this gentle queen has preserved to us a pictorial history of the Norman Conquest almost as valuable as written records. There are other royal contributors besides the good Matilda. Queen Victoria and her daughters, lineal descendants of the conqueror, have sent specimens of their handiwork wrought with both needle and brush. Her Majesty is represented by six water-color drawings, and other ladies of the royal household by paintings, knitted woolen garments and embroidery. The empresses of Russia, Austria and Germany, the queens of Italy and Spain are also among the contributors. The court laces of France and Spain and also the magnificent laces of Queen Marguerite of Italy, of priceless value, are on exhibition. The royal jewels of Queen Isabella of Spain and the sword of "Her Most Catholic Majesty" occupy a place of honor, and are guarded with zealous care. Many exquisite hand-wrought and painted tapestries done by women of our own and other lands adorn the walls. Decorative art is illustrated in all its branches. Pictures done in every medium known to artists, sculpture, wood and ivory carving, industrial and architectural drawing, all done by the hand of woman testify to her advancement in the realms of creative and practical art, and warn her brother man that he must look well to his laurels. The library too, gives indisputable evidence of woman's inherent right to occupy the field of literature, since also in this department she has "come, seen and conquered." Time would fail to mention one half the names of women writers whose works are to be found here. Harriet Martineau, George Eliot, Frances Burney, Lady Jane Grey, Miss Austen, Charlotte Bronte and hosts of others, well known to fame, are represented, some by original manuscripts.

One of the earliest books printed (1450) is attributed to Dame Juliane Barnes. It is entitled the "Boke of St. Albins," and treats of hawking, hunting and heraldry. Books in every language and from every country, written by women, are found in this well-stocked library. From Spain come the religious writings of St. Therese of Jesus, which rank among the Spanish classics.

An attractive display of French dolls, dressed to represent the costumes of American women from Puritan days to the present time, occupies a glass case near the north entrance. A similar display in the French department represents all the famous court beauties of France from the fourteenth century, in the dress belonging to the respective peri-

ods. Spain has a like exhibit, illustrating historic costumes of various classes. In the Russian department also are lay figures dressed to represent the costumes of different ranks, from elegant silk and

Hall of Honor Art Exhibit in the Woman's Building

"Pictures done in every medium known to artists, sculpture, wood and ivory carving, industrial and architectural drawing, all done by the hand of woman testify to her advancement in the realms of creative and practical art, and warns her brother man that he must look well to his laurels."

brocades heavy with gold and silver embroidery, to the simplest dress of the humblest peasant.

On the second floor are the assembly hall and president's reception room, the latter beautifully decorated by Miss Agnes Pittman of Cincinnati, and furnished by contributions from women of various states. It contains many relics, many exquisite and unique works of art. The California, Kentucky and Cincinnati rooms contain much of beauty and interest.

An exhibit of Irish laces and of the work of Scotch women are both under the charge of Lady Aberdeen, who has given a new impetus to the former industry by setting the fashion of wearing Irish lace at the castle balls.

Woman's work in various humanitarian and educational departments, and in social reform, has also its exponent. Among some of the societies represented are Kings' Daughters, Woman's Christian Temperance union, Woman's Relief Corps, Shut-In Society, College Alumnae Association, and Society for Promotion of Physical Culture.

The building is crowded with illustrations of woman's work and progress. Indeed, this crowded condition is the only criticism to be made upon it. But filled as it is, it yet does not contain all the specimens of woman's skill which the Columbian exposition has to show. In all the state buildings and in many of the foreign and main buildings, their handiwork is likewise to be found.

A few steps across the way bring us to the Children's Building, where we will linger long enough to see the provision which has been made for the care, instruction and amusement of the little folks, while their parents are viewing the fair without anxiety as to their well-being. This building provides a well protected and pleasant playground upon the roof, a gymnasium on the lower floor, where athletic exercises suitable to various ages and conditions may be engaged in, a kitchen-garden where little girls are taught to perform simple household tasks, a kindergarten where the younger ones are instructed and amused. But the most delightful feature of all is the crèche where babies are tenderly cared for by sweet-faced nurses in snowy caps and aprons. The glass doors which separate this baby's paradise from the main hall, are surrounded from morning till night by admiring crowds, pressing eagerly forward to get a glimpse of these toddling, creeping, laughing, crowing, and it must be confessed, sometimes wailing little specimens of humanity. One would suppose, from the number of admiring spectators, that babies were as rare as $100,000 diamonds, or Magnolia vases, for nowhere is there as much pushing and eager curiosity displayed as before the glass doors of this shrine of earthly cherubs. Little do the occupants of the nursery, however, care for all the admiration which they evoke. They jingle their rattles, roll their balls, suck their little fists, kick and squirm with perfect unconcern. They are not all angels, though they do inhabit a sort of paradise. If Ida May can get her fingers in little Topsy's wool, if Baby Bell wants Gretchen's rubber doll, if Johnny Boy prefers Sammy's bottle to his own, no considerations of humanity or generosity, no troublesome scruples as to "meum and tuum" will deter them from attempting to gratify their desires. If interfered with in their predatory and cruel designs, they will "lift up their voices, cry aloud and spare not." The big exposition creates no feeling of awe in their tiny breasts. What does it signify to them that this is the "biggest show on earth," that science, wisdom, skill and art have brought hither from their treasures "things new and old?" The four walls of the crèche bound their world, the patient nurses are their subjects, and they know full well that here, as in every other corner of the globe, "baby is king!" Here is "music in the air" from "morn to dewy eve." Some one has wittily dubbed the crèche "a howling success." That it is a success will testify many a grateful mother, who, in the morning, has, with many a misgiving, left her checked and ticketed darling to the care of strangers, but, after a day of untrammeled pleasure, has returned at night to find it smiling and happy, reluctant to leave its new-found Eden.

The world's fair commission never covered itself with greater glory than when it recognized the rights and needs of the little ones, and provided so delightfully for their comfort. Whatever they have done for the rest of mankind, their wise foresight has made this indeed the baby's jubilee year.

MARIAN SHAW.

WHITE CITY CHIPS

The Argus Correspondent Strolls Into the North Part of the Fair Grounds,

And Gets a Glimpse of Far-Away Japan's Pretty Group of Buildings.

Next Is Entered the Palace of Fisheries, a Place Extremely Interesting,

And an Inspection of the Federal Exhibit and Foreign Buildings Completes the Day.

CHICAGO, Oct. 29.—[Special Correspondence.]—At the northern extremity of Wooded Island, embowered in leafy shrubbery and surrounded by gardens gay with flowers, stands the unique group of buildings known as the Japanese Hoo-Den. They are bright and attractive with decorations and furnishings peculiar to the Flowery Kingdom, and altogether form one of the most charming and idyllic spots of the whole exposition. One of these pavilions represents an ancient monastery, whose history dates from 1397. From its ornamentation it takes the name "Golden Pavilion." Another is a fac-simile of the "Hoo-Den," or Phoenix hall, dating from 1052. Its shape is designed to represent the fabulous bird from which it derives its name. No iron enters into the construction of these buildings, wooden pins and bolts taking the place of nails.

The group has been presented to Chicago by the Japanese government and will remain at Jackson park.

Crossing one of the many beautiful arched bridges which span the lagoon, we see before us a simple but elegant building of the Romanesque type, surmounted by graceful turrets. Entering, we are greeted by a "very ancient and fish-like smell," and it needs no legend inscribed above the portal to tell us that we are in the Palace of Fisheries. Our eyes are greeted by a wilderness of fishing tackle, nets and poles and every implement, great and small, which is employed in coaxing the finny denizens of the seas, lakes and rivers from their hiding places, or for pursuing and capturing the mightier monsters of the deep. Fishing boats of every description are seen, manned by lay figures representing fishermen of every land and clime, so life-like that one almost listens to hear them speak. Not only is there a display of all implements employed in commercial fishing, but also of all inventions pertaining to this industry, including the science of fish farming. Everything that has ever made its home in the water, everything that "walketh through the paths of the sea," has its representative here. Corals, sea-anemones, whales, sharks, devil-fish from the briny depths of ocean—perch, sucker, trout, from brook and lake, even minnows from the shallowest stream, are in this wonderful collection.

The most interesting exhibit, however, is that of the live fish in the aquarium. No matter how deserted or neglected other exhibits of the fair may be, the tanks in which these mottled, speckled and shining beauties are disporting themselves, are always surrounded by dense and curious crowds. Here appears to be some peculiar, unexplainable attraction. As to Wordsworth's clown—

"A primrose on the river's brim,
A yellow primrose was to him,
And it was nothing more"—

so many a sight-seer has hitherto looked upon a fish as nothing but a fish. To such this display is a revelation. Here is the very poetry of motion from the lively little gold-fish darting hither and thither like streaks of yellow sunlight, to the ponderous pickerel moving with slow and stately grace. Here is the very fish from whose peculiar cast of countenance Dickens must have drawn his picture of his unctuous Mr. Pumblechoock. Here is one with the protruding lower jaw that indicates a perverse and stubborn nature. Here is one with a solemn, sanctimonious expression, that might prove a very Pecksniff among fishes. There are some with receding chins indicating a lack of firmness and decision, some with a supercilious, curled-up lip, some whose flat snouts plainly show their swinish propensities, some whose receding foreheads indicate a lack of intellect, others with broad and noble brows that might well gain them entrance to Boston's most cultured circles, whose chief requisites are said to be the possession of a high forehead and the ability to converse in Sanscrit. Whether these denizens of the deep have the latter qualification or not I cannot say; they certainly possess the first. Then there are others with sad and gloomy faces who have evidently found their aqueous world, like ours, a vale of tears. There was a big green turtle, which a young lady of our party adopted as her special pet, coming almost every day to visit him. He seemed to appreciate her attentions, and would come sailing lazily out from his refuge of rocks and sea-grasses, slowly paddling his great, ungainly form, then with a vanity known only to a homely creature who imagines itself beautiful, turn and twist its ponderous body to display itself in every conceivable attitude, and finally stretching out its long neck, as if in compliment to its admirer, with a parting wriggle of its diminutive pointed tail, would slowly paddle itself back to its retreat.

South of the Fisheries Building, separated from it by an arm of the lagoon, is the Palace of Federal Exhibits, containing displays characteristic of the various departments of government. The war department is represented by every kind of artillery and all the death-dealing implements and accoutrements that pertain to modern warfare. The merciful side of this barbarous method of adjusting national differences is shown by the model military hospital, with all its modern equipments. The equipage of camp and field is likewise shown in the display of the commissary department. There are interesting displays also from the treasury and postoffice departments. Notable among the exhibits of the latter are myriads of curious articles taken from the dead-letter office. Uncle Sam's carrier service has been made to do duty in the transmission of every conceivable kind of "portable property," from snakes and stuffed elephants to roller skates and circular saws. The U.S. geological display is of especial interest to scientists, and the relic-hunter will find pleasure in examining the famous cannon "Long Tom," the old forty-two-pound gun, which did distinguished service in the war of 1812;—in the first type-writing machine, patented in 1829, and in the postage stamp and transportation exhibits. In the latter is a model of a modern postal car, complete in all its interior as well as exterior appointments. The Sims-Edison torpedo, the largest of its kind owned by the United States war department, the "Big Tree," in whose capacious interior is a winding stairway leading to the top, the wax figures representing various North

American Indian tribes, attract universal attention. These last are so life-like that one finds them quite as interesting and, in many respects, much more agreeable than many living representatives of the noble red man scattered about the grounds.

In that portion of the park fronting the lake, and bounded on the north, west and south by the art palace, the North pond and the fisheries, are gathered the foreign buildings. They form a picturesque and interesting group, each foreign nation having attempted something characteristic in architecture and decoration. The Central and South American states successfully compete with the older European nations for honors in the line of architectural design and artistic ornamentation. Worthy of note in this respect are the structures which represent Colombia, Ecuador, Guatemala, Venezuela and Costa Rica. Brazil is represented by a building in the form of a Greek cross, combining some forms of the French renaissance, and uniting elegance with solidity. It is sixty feet high, surmounted by a dome measuring ninety feet above the roof. The roof is also adorned with a beautiful garden of tropical plants. The interior is decorated with bas reliefs, sculptures and paintings representative of the country's history. The chief exhibit is coffee. The fantastic sky-line of the German building, the bell-shaped wooden dome of the Swedish, and the indescribably comical roof of the Norwegian add to the picturesqueness of the scene. In the Turkish pavilion, the most noticeable feature is the open spindle-work used so freely in its decoration. The outer walls are divided into panels by beams carved with sentences from the Koran. The panels set in spindle-work are bright with yellow and reddish brown. In the corners are fan shaped panels of mother-of-pearl. France presents a graceful and massive palace adorned with artistic groups of statuary and exquisite friezes, whose motive is a trades procession. England shows a manor house of simple Tudoresque style. Few of the foreign buildings contain extensive exhibits, many of them being used merely as headquarters for the various foreign commissions.

MARIAN SHAW.

PALACE OF ART

Sketch of Some of the Wonderful Works in Sculpture and Painting at the Fair.

America Represented by 1,006 Paintings in Oil, and 2,000 Etchings and Pastels.

Works of Corot, Millet, Delacroix and Other Famous Masters in the Loan Exhibit.

Artists From Every Nation Compete—Verdict of the Visitor to the Exposition.

CHICAGO, Oct. 30—[Special Correspondence.]—The thousand forms of art displayed in the great Palace of Manufactures are most of them produced by machinery. The embroideries, laces, etc., of the Woman's Building, the carvings, lacquer and decorative work seen there and elsewhere, the wonders wrought in metals, the grand and costly achievements of ceramics—all go under the general name of applied arts. That Art which is written with a capital A and is called high art, consists of the various forms of sculpture and painting and has its apotheosis in the Palace of Fine Arts.

Here the United States exhibits 1,006 paintings in oil with nearly 2,000 etchings, water-colors and pastels. This includes the collection of foreign masterpieces owned in our country, and the retrospective exhibit of American paint-ing, which shows our progress in art from the pioneer days of West, Peale and Allston down to the present time.

The foreign or loan collection includes twelve Corots, twelve Millets, three paintings by Delacroix, the father of the French romantic school, one by Courbet, the father of French realism, and one by Ingres, the brightest modern exponent of the classic school. Most of these paintings are French, but Germany, Holland and Belgium are represented by the great painters, Von Uhde, Israels, Baron Leys and Van Beers, while Alma Tadema, John M. Swan and George Watts uphold the fair fame of England. This is the finest collection of masterpieces ever made.

Notable among canvases of the United States section are George Fuller's "Quadroon," Edwin Blashfield's "Angel with the Flaming Sword," and "Christmas Bells." The latter, marvelous in coloring and exquisite in conception, portrays a band of bright-robed angels ringing out the glad tidings of a Saviour's birth.

"The Days That Are No More" is lovely and pathetic. There are two "Judgments of Paris," one a dignified work by the late Henry Gray, where real goddesses contend for a real golden apple; the other a burlesque where a Dutch boor deliberates as to which of two very ugly girls he shall give the yellow pippin he holds in his hand. Other paintings by this same artist, Walter McEwen, a western man, are "The Ghost Story," and "The Absent One on All Souls' Day."

Another western painter, Gari Melchers of Detroit, has seven remarkable pictures, most admired of which are "The Communion," "The Sermon," and "Married."

Carl Marr of Wisconsin has the distinction of painting the most ghastly, gory and sensational picture of the

American exhibit. It is "The Flagellants," and depicts a scene in Florence during the religious sway of Savonarola, a procession of men and women lashing themselves over the naked shoulders and bleeding from the gaping wounds, while one of their number in a dying state is borne along on a litter. These three western painters have had Munich and Paris training.

In pleasing contrast to "The Flagellants," is Thomas Hovenden's charming domestic scene, "Bringing Home the Bride." This artist enjoys the honor of having painted the most popular picture of the world's fair. "Breaking Home Ties" is its title. In pathos, naturalness and that human sympathy that makes the whole world kin, this picture is a masterpiece. Strong men stand before it with tears that do not belie their manhood—for this mother parting with her boy who is going forth to wrestle with a hard, up-hill world, recalls a moving chapter in their own boyhood.

S. E. Weeks in "Three Beggars of Cordova" and "The Last Voyage" also touches chords that vibrate in every sympathetic heart.

Mr. Whistler, an American artist who is better known in London and Paris than at home, exhibits six oil paintings which are in his eccentric yet fascinating style. "The Lady with the Yellow Buskin" and "The Princess of the Land of Porcelain" are the fanciful titles of two of them. But most famous of his works are sixty-three etchings, said to be the finest since Rembrandt.

Throughout this entire collection, American art shows itself dominated by French influence, and leans strongly toward impressionism.

One story-telling picture in the Canada section attracts all eyes. Its title is "The Foreclosure of the Mortgage." The foreclosure takes place in the humble home where a father lies sick unto death, where a mother weeps in despair, while wistful-eyed children scan questioningly the stern face of the officer of the law, and a dazed old grandmother rocks mechanically the cradle of an infant who sleeps on smiling and happy in blissful ignorance.

Great Britain in its two galleries shows the best work of native living artists. This whole art exposition, it may be remarked in passing, belongs to the living and not to the dead. Sir Frederic Leighton, president of the London Royal Academy, has three mythological paintings: "The Garden of the Hesperides," "Perseus and Andromeda" and "Hercules Wrestling With Death for the Body of Alcestes." "The Roll Call," a famous picture by Lady Butler, is lent by the queen. "The Last Muster" and "Entranced" show Hubert Herkomer at his best. Leslie of the Royal Academy has "A Hen and Chickens," real as in life, and a very sweet "Home Sweet Home." "The Passing of Arthur," "The Birth of Venus," "Old Sea Dogs at Tresport," "The Redemption of Tannhauser" and "Christ and the Magdalen" are masterpieces which once seen can never be forgotten. The achievement of all English speaking lands in sculpture, shows nothing finer than the "Death and the Sculptor" of our American artist, Daniel C. French.

In the vast and marvelous French section, sculpture occupies the highest place. "Quand Même" typifies the spirit of Alsace and Lorraine in defeat, by a young girl, who with one arm supports a soldier who has died in their defense, and with the other grasps defiantly the musket that has fallen from his hand. "Gloria Victis" a marble group of ideal loveliness, exalts the blessedness of those who lay down life for country, by showing a dead soldier borne to Elysium in the arms of a beneficent goddess. In "The Siren" who carries off a little child, frightened and yet entranced, and "The Spirit Guarding the Secret of the Tomb," with attitude of awe and face veiled in mystery; in "Jesus Before the Rabbis" and "The Nymph With a Shell," one sees examples of all that is best and highest in modern sculpture.

From the 730 paintings of this section which embrace an infinite variety of subjects treated in every style, we can single out only a few—"The Annunciation," "The Guardian Angel," "Young St. John," "In Wonderland" and Bougereau's adorable masterpiece, "The Holy Women at the Tomb." Here at the empty sepulchre, we see the angel of the Lord, "with countenance like lightning and raiment white as snow," announcing to Salome and the two Marys the joyful tidings, "He is not here. He is risen!"

Germany's great collection excels that of France in strength, seriousness and grandeur, though as a whole inferior to it in beauty. Among its finest sculptures are: "A Sleeping Child," "A Resting Boy," "Victory" and "Andromeda."

In painting, several "Ave Maria's" dispute the palm of beauty, while the "Christmas Evening" and "Announcement to the Shepherds" of the celebrated Von Uhde, show that modern as well as ancient painters find their highest inspiration in sacred themes.

The greatest painters of the Munich and Dusseldorf schools contribute to this grand display, while the national gallery of Berlin and the state of Bavaria send to it many of their rarest treasures. Among these national paintings we recall "Apotheosis," "Queen Louise," "Revery," "Inundation," "A Summer Landscape" and "Twilight."

Russia's display is a marvel and a revelation to those who have looked upon the vast empire of the Czar as but one remove from barbarism. Ivan Con-stantinovich's five large canvases depicting various scenes in the life of Columbus, attract much attention from their powerful drawing, and luminous effects. His "Naples by Moonlight" seems like a glimpse into fairy land. Makovsky's "Bride's Attire," "Portrait of a Lady" and "Romeo and Juliet" are surpassed in ideal loveliness by no picture in the exposition. "For Christ's Sake," "Easter Hallowe'en," "The Candle-Bearers" and "Christ in the House of Lazarus" are pictures of entrancing beauty. Most of the paintings in this superb collection are the property of the Imperial Academy. "The Cossack's Answer," which has been loaned by the emperor, is pronounced by critics the artistic gem of the collection.

The Society of Polish Artists makes a wonderful display, strong and full of that pathos inseparably connected with the art and history of this chivalrous but conquered nation. "Therig Segismund's Vision" is divine. "Milda" is worthy of her name as goddess of love. In "A Rustic Astronomer," a country boy enveloped in the deep blue shadows of a moonless night, lies prone on the grass of a lonely meadow and seeks to pierce the mystery of the starry heavens. "Harvest in Sandomir," "The Four Seasons" and "Ophelia" are beautiful, while "Under the Influence of Hasheesh" depicts two young women who have succumbed to the fatal drug, and whose ghastly beauty is in striking contrast to the vivid splendor of their surroundings. "After the Storm" is the masterpiece of this collection.

The Holland gallery which includes the works of such famous Dutch painters as the four Mesdags and Josef Israels, needs no words of praise. "Alone in the World," Israels' great picture, has received the first prize of the exposition art jury. It represents a man sitting by the bedside of his dead wife, and tells that story of loss and loneliness with the consummate art possible only to the highest genius. Other works of this section show that the old land of Rembrandt and Rubens has in our day had a renaissance of art.

"St. Cecelia Singing," "Poverella" and "Sweet Slumber" are among the many lovely sculptures of the Belgian exhibit. "The Departure of the Herd" and "The Road Through the Dunes" are lovely companion landscapes with sheep in motion, and as natural as life. "Peace" is an idyllic scene laid in that good time coming, when the nations shall learn war no more. "The Last Days of Pompeii" depicts even more vividly than Bulwer's masterly romance, the tragedy of a city's destruction.

The number and excellence of Italy's works of art, allows only slight mention. M. Bardi has twelve sculptures, four of which typify Europe, Asia, America and Africa. Finest of them all is the "Angel of the Resurrection." "Pereat" shows two beautiful women at a gladiatorial contest. To one of them, a royal lady, is given the choice of life or death for the vanquished combatant in the arena. By turning down the thumb she decrees his death. Finer than even Millet's "Angelus" seems "The Angelus on St. Peter's Day" of this collection. "The Bay of Naples," "Sunset at Venice" and scores of other triumphs of landscape and figure painting, realize the highest ideals of art and beauty.

Spain has a few excellent sculptures. "The Last Hurrah," "The Embarkation of Columbus," "The Sisters of Charity," "Another Marguerite" and "The Arts Saluting Immortality," show the worthy trend of modern painting in the ancient land of Velasquez and Murillo.

"Lady Macbeth Walking in Her Sleep," "A Danaid" and a "Girl Making Pottery" are recalled as fine examples of Danish sculpture. In painting, "Three

Old Fellows,""In the Child's Home," "A Dead Calm," "Job and His Friends" and "Cain" will be remembered; but "Worn Out" is the most impressive piece of this collection. It portrays a man fallen prostrate from hard work in a lone harvest field, while the old wife stands by sad and helpless.

Sweden's most popular painter of today is Anders Zorn. His pictures in the Swedish gallery are "Margit," "Omnibus," "Ball," "Fair in Mora," "A Young Study" and "A Toast in Idun." Idun is the Swedish goddess of youth, and this toast is drank at an aesthetic club of Stockholm named in her honor. Zorn accompanied his pictures to Chicago, and there as at his home in Stockholm, people rave over him. His royal highness, Prince Eugen of Sweden and Norway has three paintings in his deeply mystical and poetic style. They are "The Forest," "Autumn Day" and "The Temple."

While Swedish art closely follows French models, and has gone daft over impressionism, Norwegian art shows an originality bold and rugged as its own mountains. Normann's "Summer Night" and "North Winds on the Norway Coast," "Christmas Eve" and "An Invalid," are works of ideal refinement and beauty. This whole collection combines romance and poetry with the sternness and pathos of real life. Its most noted painting is "The Son of Man" where Christ is represented in the garb of a common working man.

Austria's sculptures are mostly mythological or portrait busts of great men. In Hans Makart, this country claims to have an artist who has painted the greatest picture the world has seen in 200 years. It is "Caterina Carnare." As it is deemed too precious for foreign transportation, it is not in Chicago. But we see this great painter in a panel picture where five beautiful women repre-

*Administration Building with Columbus Statue by Mary T. Lawrence
and Four Elements Sculptures by Karl Bitter*

"* * * its magnificent and noble palaces of marble whiteness adorned with
the best that the nineteenth century can produce of bold relief
and graceful sculpture, form a never-to-be
forgotten vision of beauty."

sent the five senses, and in a yet more exquisite masterpiece, called "The Falconer." Munkaczy, whose great painting "Christ Before Pilate" is well known in this country, has here one picture, "The Story of the Hero." Defregger, Austria's other great living painter, is in evidence with two fine paintings, "Children Playing with a Dog" and "God Bless You." The emperor has loaned to this exhibit some of the chefs d'oeuvre of his private collection.

Jamaica, Costa Rica, British Guiana and Algeria, each sends its tribute of painting and sculpture, worthy of extended mention did space permit. Brazil has contributed one splendid masterpiece, a marble group called "Christ and the Adultress." Japan makes here the first great exhibit in high art. Her paintings are rich in color and admirable in technique, but have the usual national defect in perspective. Some marvelous work in bronze shows a high order of genius combined with infinite patience. Great things in art may be hoped for from that distant realm.

When the Queen of Sheba came from

the uttermost parts of the earth to see the splendor and glory of Solomon's kingdom, her "spirit grew faint within her,"and she declared,—"It was a true report that I heard in mine own land, how be it I believed it not,—but behold the half was not told me." Such is the verdict of the visitor to the Columbian exposition. No pen can worthily describe, no pencil portray, no camera reproduce its beauties. Its location, overlooking the majestic and beautiful Lake Michigan, the plan of its grounds, diversified by canals, ponds and lagoon, its lovely lawns gemmed with rare and brilliant flowers, its magnificent and noble palaces of marble whiteness adorned with the best that the nineteenth century can produce of bold relief and graceful sculpture, form a never-to-be-forgotten vision of beauty. Whether kissed by the glowing beams of the summer sun, or lighted at night by the soft radiance of myriads of incandescent lamps, it presents always the same spectacle of wondrous beauty. This marvel of loveliness, which sprang up as under the wand of an enchanter, in a few short weeks will have vanished. Over its ruins, as above the ashes of the once fair city of Aeneas, will be written the sad legend *"Troja fuit."* The foot of the spoiler is already upon its soil, and soon these—

> "Cloud-capped towers, the gorgeous palaces,
> The solemn temples—shall dissolve,—
> And, like this unsubstantial pageant faded,
> Leave not a rack behind."

Yet, like a pleasant dream or a sweet poem, it will ever be present to our mental vision, and being "a thing of beauty," it will be "a joy forever."

Not only as a thing of beauty will its influence remain with us. The practical lessons which it has taught are of inestimable value. It will give a new impetus to commerce, science and art, it will cement more firmly the bonds of human brotherhood, it will hasten the fulfillment of our beloved Whittier's prophecy—

> "The zones unite, the poles agree,
> The tongues of striving cease;
> As on the sea of Galilee
> The Christ is whispering—'Peace!' "

MARIAN SHAW.

The last of the excellent letters from the pen of Marian Shaw will be found in today's Argus. The series of letters by Miss Shaw which have been running in The Argus are acknowledged to be among the best published anent the fair.

THE SEARCH FOR MARIAN SHAW

The series of twelve newspaper articles upon which this book is based were found in a Minneapolis rummage sale during the early 1960's. These articles, which carried the byline of Marian Shaw, were clipped from pages of 1893 newspapers, neatly pasted into a small booklet, and then carefully edited and titled in a Spencerian handwriting. The booklet also included several line drawings reminiscent of the Fair. Nearly thirty years were to pass before we considered the articles for publication, to coincide with the 500th anniversary of the first voyage of Christopher Columbus and the 100th anniversary of the 1893 World's Columbian Exposition in Chicago.

We read the articles and found them worthy. But to explain the author's background and credentials all we had to go on was her name, and the name of the newspaper in which the series of articles ran. That newspaper was called *The Argus*, but there was no city or state mentioned. A review of old newspaper directories revealed that many newspapers with this name were published during the 1890's on daily, semi-weekly and weekly schedules. Our research turned up *The Argus* as a newspaper in cities as diverse as Cleveland, Ohio; Albany, New York; Minneapolis, Minnesota; and Rock Island, Illinois, and we were able to verify that the articles were not from these places. A close reading of the articles disclosed, however, that the author had seemed to pay undue attention to the Dakotas. This, and clues in several other published references provided us with a partial breakthrough. We thereupon undertook to drive from St. Paul to Fargo, North Dakota to review old newspaper and library files. The fact that our drive was severely hindered by a late spring blizzard seemed appropriate.

In Fargo we learned that one Major Alanson W. Edwards had founded several of North Dakota's early newspapers: the *Republican*, the *Forum*, and *The Argus*. *The Argus* appeared in daily, weekly and Sunday editions starting in 1879 and continued until its merger in 1896 with the *Forum*. We also discovered that after a fire destroyed the printing plant of *The Argus* in 1886, Major Edwards rebuilt the newspaper and then struggled unsuccessfully with the resulting debts. In 1891 the railroad tycoon of St. Paul, James J. Hill, who had acquired a mortgage on the assets of *The Argus*, foreclosed on his debt. Hill appointed as the new managing editor George K. Shaw, the brother of Marian Shaw. Shaw took over his duties during October, 1891, and was fired from his post in January, 1894. Our research disclosed that the Sunday issues of *The Argus* carried serialized novels, travel articles similar in style to the articles of Marian Shaw, as well as numerous line drawings. In October, 1892 the weekly edition had 1,336 subscribers, and the Sunday paper had

1,800 subscribers. Unfortunately, all examples of *The Argus* from early June, 1893 through December 31, 1893, covering the datelines noted in the Shaw articles, have been lost. Thus, no direct comparison of the twelve articles with existing microfilms of *The Argus* was possible. However all clues, including the page layout, the type font, the style of presentation, and the fact that the managing editor was the brother of the author, indicate that this was in fact the correct *Argus* newspaper.

Being partially frustrated in our newspaper search, we turned to the usual library references. There we located two citations listing works by Marian Shaw. The first reference was to *Queen Bess, Or, What's In A Name*, published by G. P. Putnam's Sons in 1885. Further search actually turned up a book review in *The New York Times* which termed this work "a story of schoolboy love." However, a telephone inquiry about Miss Shaw to the Putnam-Berkeley Group, the publishing successors of the old G. P. Putnam's Son imprint, brought polite laughter, "She's probably not on our current backlist, is she?" and a negative reply. The second reference was even more obscure, to *Latin Prose Composition For Cicero Classes*, published in 1899 by the Minneapolis Board of Education, of which the Library of Congress has the only extant copy. This reference suggested that Miss Shaw probably had Minnesota connections, and a review of the index to the old *Minneapolis Journal* turned up her obituary. From this information, and from a search of probate and real estate records as well as documents in the Minnesota Historical Society, we were able to put together a fairly complete description of a once respected but now totally forgotten woman author and journalist. In 1900, for example, the *Minneapolis Journal* ran a series of fourteen articles on the achievements of "Minneapolis' Literary Women." One of these articles featured both Marian Shaw and her sister Frances Shaw.

Marian E. Shaw was born in 1851. She was a member of a very prominent family who traced their New World roots to the first ship to arrive after the Mayflower. John Shaw, Marian's father, had brought his wife and children west in 1851. Leaving his wife and family in Galena, Illinois, Shaw joined the settlers travelling by steamboat to the Rollingstone colony, north of Winona,

Nameplate of the Sunday Fargo Argus, of Fargo, North Dakota.

Minnesota. Shaw arrived in the early spring of 1852 and staked out his homestead. Although it had been argued that Minnesota had too cold a climate for apple growing, Shaw planted the apple seeds he had brought with him in a nail keg from Maine. Almost 300 of the 490 settlers died during their first year in Minnesota, and among the dead was John Shaw. His apple trees survived in the orchards of other settlers, however, and Shaw has been credited with having first introduced this fruit to Minnesota.

After the death of John Shaw, his wife Frances opened a boarding house in Galena, Illinois, to partially support her family. John Melvil Shaw (1833-1897), Marian's oldest brother read the law and then opened his law practice in Platteville, Wisconsin, barely twenty miles north of the then family home in Galena, Illinois. George K. Shaw (1842-1915), another brother, moved to Platteville as well, becoming the editor of the *Platteville Witness* newspaper. Both brothers then joined the Union army during the Civil War, leaving Frances Shaw (1830-1913), Marian's older sister, to run the newspaper. After the war had ended, presumably because of the connections of her brothers and sister there, Marian Shaw attended the Platteville Normal School, Wisconsin's first school for teacher training. Her course of study included mathematics, grammar, composition and rhetoric, reading and spelling, natural sciences, and U. S. history and government. Miss Shaw's previous education had been received at home and in the German language schools of Galena, Illinois. Both the Platteville school records and the United States census of 1870 carry Miss Shaw's first name as "Mary." It is probable that she changed her name to "Marian" during her early career as a public school teacher.

When he returned from military service John Melvil Shaw married a girl from a prominent Minneapolis family, and he opened his law practice there. George K. Shaw followed his brother to Minnesota, joining the staff of the newly established *Minneapolis Tribune*. While John Melvil Shaw spent the

Miss Marian Shaw

remainder of his legal career and life in Minneapolis, his brother George (frequently called the Major, after his Civil War rank) was far more peripatetic. He worked for newspapers in Minneapolis, St. Paul, Bay City (Michigan), Fargo and eventually moved to New York City. The remainder of the Shaw family also moved to Minneapolis. Marian had four sisters: Frances, a writer and translator in her own right; Clara (1841-1921), an artist; Emily, an invalid who died in 1885; and Ellen, who later married and moved to Eldora, Iowa. Perhaps as an indication of things to come, Marian Shaw was already identified as a "writer of stories" in the United States census of 1870.

In 1873 Marian Shaw was hired by the Minneapolis Public Schools as a grade school teacher, and eventually became principal of the senior class and teacher of Latin and German at the old Minneapolis Central High School, where she remained until her death in 1901. Towards the end of her career Marian Shaw was often absent from her classes due to illness. On the last day of her life the school administrator informed Miss Shaw that her services were no longer needed. According to one obituary she then returned home, became ill, and died during the night from the "nervous shock." Her brother George, then the associate editor of the *Minneapolis Tribune*, felt that this treatment amounted to murder, and a rival newspaper, the *Minneapolis Journal* so reported in its typically sensational style.

There was obviously time during school summer vacations for Miss Shaw also to pursue a writing career. In one obituary George Shaw was quoted as saying that the *Boston Evening Transcript* newspaper had published a series of Marian Shaw's letters describing the World's Industrial and Cotton Centenary Exposition of New Orleans of 1884. But how was it that the following year an obscure midwestern foreign language teacher could also be published by the important firm of G. P. Putnam's Sons? Marian Shaw's sister Frances may well have helped find this publisher, as she then resided in Boston. Alternately, there may have been a contact made through a Boston lawyer, Herbert Putnam, the publisher's son, who came to Minneapolis in 1884 to work at the Minneapolis Athenaeum. Herbert Putnam served as the city's first librarian until 1892, when he returned to Boston. Later he was to direct the Boston Public Library and then the Library of Congress.

The Woman's building at the Chicago World's Fair contained in its library over 7,000 volumes written by women, collected by committees in many states and foreign countries. Also exhibited were photographs and biographical sketches of these authors. Among these materials was a typewritten pamphlet, entitled *Minnesota Literature: Minneapolis* which described some of the State's then active women writers. The pages for Marian Shaw indicate that she wrote "mainly in the line of fiction, but she has won success in journalism as an occasional editorial writer, correspondent and essayist." Ready for publication, this pamphlet indicated, were "two very bright short stories entitled 'Mrs. Billings' Spring House: a Story of a Quaint Old Town,' and 'The Little Intruder.'" Regretfully, it has not been possible to locate either of these stories, in print or in manuscript.

Marian's sister, Frances, was mentioned in another publication produced for the Fair, which concerned Minnesota women journalists. An essay for that booklet, written by Lillie Merrick Yeatman, the women's editor for the *Minneapolis Times*, noted that Minneapolis had more women employed on newspaper staffs than any other city of comparable size. Miss Yeatman felt, however, that if she could advise any would-be journalists, she would caution them "stick to type-writing, dress-making, cooking or teaching, they at least are sure, and pay fully as well."

The obituaries of Marian Shaw also indicated that among her other published essays and stories were "Miss Winchester's Will" and "Those Horrid Boys," both of which ran as serials. Unfortunately, we have been unable to locate these references either, as the indexing to magazines of the Victorian era is only rudimentary at best. It is reported, incidentally, that these two serials, as well as her 1885 novel *Queen Bess*, were exhibited in the library of the Woman's Building at the Chicago World's Fair. Miss Shaw had also prepared leaflets on Latin prose and reading Virgil at sight, as well as leaving in manuscript form at the time of her death a complete translation of the *Odes of Horace*, a volume of short stories, and several longer studies. One obituary indicated that Miss Shaw's sister, Frances, a member of the prestigious New England Club (which was organized by Julia Ward Howe and included among its prominent women author members Louisa May Alcott) would edit and publish these manuscripts. However, no further library references to these works have been located, and inquiries to Marian Shaw's few remaining collateral descendants have turned up no further record.

That the untimely passing of Marian Shaw was a shock to the local community can be ascertained by a review of the Minneapolis newspapers at the time of her death on April 19, 1901. Her photograph appeared in two newspapers, and one is reproduced in this chapter. School was dismissed and the flag at the top of the Central High School building was lowered to half staff. The senior class and teachers of Central High School also attended her funeral as a group. Additionally, the Minneapolis Teachers Club resolved, "In the death of Miss Shaw a noble life has gone out and the teaching force of this city has suffered an irreparable loss." The obituaries noted that at the time of her promotion to principal of the senior class room, she was presented a statue and a testimonial which concluded: "We look upon your advancement to this position as a victory. Symbolizing this, we have brought you a Winged Victory to perch upon your table, and we hope it may remind you of our appreciation of your work in connection with the public schools of the city." It is interesting to note that a large replica of the statue of the Winged Victory stood on the dome of the Fine Arts building at the Chicago Fair. Miss Shaw's former students who were attending the University of Minnesota also wrote a testimonial in her memory for the college newspaper, the *Minnesota Daily*.

What brought Marian Shaw to write about the Chicago World's Fair? It has been convincingly argued that the various world's fairs, commencing with the 1876 Centennial Exposition in Philadelphia, broadened the opportunities for women in journalism. Speaking about the 1876 Exposition in the book, *What America Owes To Women*, which was written as a national exposition souvenir for the Chicago World's Fair, Susan E. Dickinson wrote:

> Many women began their journalistic work as correspondents there for papers scattered all over the country, giving graphic accounts of what was to be seen at the great fair for readers who could not go thither. To-day women form the majority of foreign correspondents. Their letters from every corner almost of Europe and many of Asia, and often from South American countries, from Mexico, and from our own western "frontier" towns, have become too familiar to the reading public to excite surprise or comment that it is a woman who is taking adventurous or perilous journeys and recording events and scenery.

That Marian Shaw was already qualified as a travel journalist is clear from her previously published letters in the *Boston Evening Transcript* about the New Orleans Fair. The management of *The Argus* was obviously convinced of this as well, for her last published letter about the Chicago Fair was followed with this laudatory statement:

> The last of the excellent letters from the pen of Marian Shaw will be found in today's Argus. The series of letters by Miss Shaw which have been running in The Argus are acknowledged to be among the best published anent the fair.

The erudition which the Minneapolis Latin teacher displays in her articles is striking, considering that she attended a frontier teachers' college for only one year. For example, Miss Shaw cites in her August 18 article the comments of the Reverend F. Herbert Stead. Stead visited the Fair in May of 1893 and his commentary appeared in the July, 1893 issue of *The Review of Reviews*. This literary magazine was very important at the time. In her October 13 article, headlined "CAGED LIGHTNING," Ms. Shaw quotes portions of the first three verses of "The Song of the Lightning" by George W. Cutter. In her October 29 article headed "WHITE CITY CHIPS" the reference to a primrose comes from Part One of William Wordsworth's poem "Peter Bell." In her final article, dated October 30th, Marian Shaw refers to a speech by Prospero contained in Act IV, Scene I of Shakespeare's *The Tempest*. The concluding lines of that same article came from John Greenleaf Whittier's poem about the transatlantic cable, entitled "The Cable Hymn," which is part of a longer work known as *The Tent on the Beach*.

There is also a tantalizing reference in the Minneapolis Central High School student yearbook of 1892 to a visit by the graduating class to the Art building at the Chicago World's Fair. While this reference is probably hyperbole only, since that class graduated before the Fair opened, still the subject was undoubtedly on the minds of Miss Shaw and her students.

Long before Marian Shaw wrote her series of articles, midwestern newspapers had printed information about the Fair. Financial, political and construction news appeared in the months before opening day. Later, lists of those who had attended the Fair were mixed with hints for travellers yet to attend. A dispatch printed in the July 6, 1893 *Scott County Argus* of Shakopee, Minnesota commented that fairgoers should bathe each day, wear light and comfortable clothing, and be careful what they ate or drank. "If ice cream soda or other cold drinks are taken, they should be indulged in moderately, drank slowly, very deliberately, and the party had better seat himself while drinking." Thus, Marian Shaw hardly needed, as she noted, to repeat much of the factual information which had already appeared.

Speaking of early promotional efforts for the Chicago World's Fair, it was reported that "every week some 23,000 letters, circulars, and pamphlets were mailed to the various states . . . " Newspaper clippings were also made and distributed at the rate of many million words a day. By March, 1893 this volume of correspondence and communication had, according to historian Hubert Howe Bancroft, assumed enormous proportions, the mail matter amounted to 50,000 to 60,000 pieces, including more than 20,000 journals. The first U. S. picture postcards also made their appearance at the Fair.

Marian Shaw might well have taken advantage of one of the many special excursions or trips offered for Minnesotans to visit the Fair. For example, the *Minneapolis Journal* offered special four day tours to Chicago for the Fair, which included railroad fare, meals, and hotel rooms, for a cost between $14.75 and $15.60. Visitors to the Minnesota building were encouraged to sign the guest register, and Miss Shaw's signature can be found on the pages dated July 20 and 27, 1893. The registration indicated that she and her sisters stayed at a small hotel at 5203 Madison Avenue, very close to the fairgrounds.

The management of the Fair also went out of its way to assist visiting journalists such as Marian Shaw. Special rooms in the department of Promotion and Publicity were devoted to the press. According to Bancroft, "In describing the wonders of the Exposition, some of the ablest pens are busied, representing nearly all our states and territories, with many foreign lands, and forming probably the largest gathering of correspondents ever seen." Indeed, "they are giving," said author Trumbull White, "their efforts to the record of its wonders in newspapers and magazines and volumes."

It has been said that, at best, the documentation of women's history is a treasure hunt. That such is the case can be clearly seen from our efforts to search for Marian Shaw.

There are also several layers of meaning which can be gleaned from the Shaw articles. It is clear that she was excited and literally stood in awe before the universe of mankind's achievements which the Fair had gathered together. This sense of wonderment was what Ms. Shaw tried to convey to her readers. What she stressed in her comments and descriptions obviously reflected her own background. As she was a sister of Union Army veterans, the Krupp guns, "those monster engines of destruction," repelled her as they evoked military memories. The grains and grasses in midwestern displays were familiar even though woven in "fantastic and beautiful forms," but the "bewildering display" of oranges and lemons must have seemed as exotic as the Midway Plaisance to this Latin teacher from Minneapolis. Such fruits were rare indeed in Minnesota in the 1890's.

Marian Shaw's last article deals with the Midway, that same area whose noise and smells bothered her when she had first entered the fairgrounds. Although she had heard that this area afforded opportunities for ethnographic study or could even replace foreign travel, Marian Shaw was not convinced. She was not sure that some of the exhibits were any more typical of their countries than Buffalo Bill was of the United States.

Marian Shaw was fascinated by the displays of machinery, by inventions such as the Yerkes telescope (whose image she pasted on the cover of her booklet), by the fine and applied arts, and most of all, by the spectacle of the "White City." She felt proud and patriotic after visiting the various state buildings, but, like many others, it was the lighting of the Fair which drew her highest praise. The arc and incandescent lamps, the great searchlight, and the electric powered fountains, especially at night, created glorious beauty which "strikes the beholder dumb." Such electrical technology had barely come to her home state.

Ms. Shaw was but one of many women journalists who wrote about the World's Columbian Exposition. In her chapter "Women and the Press," Dr. Ann Feldman writes about the opportunities which the Fair offered to women writers and discusses some of the noteworthy related events which occurred during the Fair's six month history. While scholars have analyzed the effect which the Fair has had on urban planning, fair and park design, and even on the development of department stores, the role of the Fair in the history of women's journalism is clearly less known. The discovery of Marian Shaw's small booklet of articles has led not only to the rediscovery of a forgotten writer, but to an important analysis by Dr. Feldman of the emerging world of women's journalism of which Marian Shaw was once a part.

WOMEN AND THE PRESS AT THE 1893 WORLD'S COLUMBIAN EXPOSITION

The 1893 World's Columbian Exposition attracted over 27 million visitors primarily through print media. In addition to the voluminous publications of the Fair's Department of Publicity, daily newspapers, magazines, and journals nationwide covered the wrangling between New York, Chicago, and St. Louis about hosting the Fair, the choice of Chicago as the Fair site, the construction of the buildings, and the actual six-month exposition, making the Fair of international interest even before it opened.[1] Not only was the Fair a news item for the press, but several journalists recognized the power of the press in drawing the enormous crowds. Teresa Dean (d.1935), a reporter for the Chicago *Inter-Ocean*, wrote:

> See here, World's Fair directors, and commissioners, and managers, do you not think it about time you stopped patting each other on the back . . . to thank the Chicago press for what it has done for you? . . . It has made the World's Fair what it has been in the present and what it will be in history. It has brought millions through the turn-stiles where only thousands would have come.[2]

Dean was one of several women reporters and editors who contributed not only to the publicity for the 1893 Fair, but participated in the Woman's Building and in women's congresses featuring the press. The prominence and strength of newspaperwomen at this Fair was the result of nearly forty years of advances for women in the field. By presenting here an overview of the historical background of presswomen in the United States in that period with short biographies of outstanding women reporters and editors, the stage can be set for the strong role of women and the press at the 1893 Fair.

Women newspaper journalists, free lance contributors, editors and publishers had become increasingly prominent in the latter half of the nineteenth century. In 1870, out of a total of 5,286 earning their living in daily journalism, 35 were women.[3] By 1880 the number of women had increased to 288 and by 1890 there were 600 more.[4] These census numbers did not include the many women contributing occasional articles to newspapers and magazines, or women authors and poets.

"Jennie June" (Jane Cunningham) Croly (1829-1901) was the first woman to work full time for a daily newspaper, and as early as 1857 was the first woman to syndicate her material. In 1862 she took over the woman's department of the *New York World*, and in 1872 went over to the *Daily Graphic* as an editor. C. T. Evans, an associate who wrote her memorial in *The New York Times*, described her articles:

Teresa Dean

They were written by a woman for women . . . the maids and matrons of the country . . . who have never before been so addressed by one of their sex—a woman they came to know and to hold in highest esteem.[5]

Croly began the first major woman's club after being barred from an 1868 reception and banquet given by the New York Press Club for Charles Dickens. This club was named the Sorosis, for which she enlisted writer Alice Cary, journalists Kate Field and "Fanny Fern" (Sara Payson Willis Parton, 1811-1872), and editor Ellen Demorest as members. The word "sorosis" was Greek, meaning the sweet flavor of many fruits, indicating the diversity of its membership and the "sweetness" of joining together. One of the first activities of this club was to host a tea for the Press Club during which the women spoke and the men had to listen.[6] In 1889 Jennie June helped found both the Woman's Press Club and the General Federation of Women's Clubs. The combination of press and club work was carried on in her role as editor of the *New Cycle* of the General Federation of Women's Clubs.

The idea of a paper to promote the cause of women was not new. Equal rights for women were promoted through the *Lily* (1849-1856), the *Agitator* (1858-1869), *Revolution* (1868-1872), the *Woman's Journal* (1870-1917) and the *Women's Tribune* (1883-1909). The *Union Signal* (begun in 1875) was the organ of the Woman's Christian Temperance Union (W.C.T.U.) Other business and professional women's organizations, like the Association of Collegiate Alumnae (begun in 1888), also had their own journals.

African-American women, too, made their mark in the "negro press." Among the newspapers and periodicals promoting the causes of interest to this constituency were the *New York Freeman*, the Chicago *Conservator*, and the *A.M.E. Review*. The most prominent African-American female journalist was Ida B. Wells who first wrote under the pen name of "Iola."

Ida B. Wells (1862-1931) was the child of slaves, and was orphaned at the age of 16. After teaching to support her family, she then became a journalist and editor. Her specialty was race reporting, stressing the brutality of attacks on Afro-Americans, and the

Jennie June Croly

85

prevalence of lynching. At the 1887 National Afro-American Press convention she was named assistant secretary for the group and acclaimed as its most prominent correspondent.[7] After a few years of contributing articles to various newspapers including *The Living Way* in Memphis, she became a part-owner of the *Memphis Free Speech* in 1892. In March of that year, three friends of hers were lynched in Memphis. She not only demanded the trial and conviction of the murderers, but recommended an economic boycott by Afro-Americans. During a trip out of town, a mob wrecked her newspaper plant and Wells joined the staffs of the *New York Age* and the Chicago *Conservator*.

By 1889, women had made such an impact on the profession that the professional journal, *The Journalist*, devoted its entire January 26 issue to profiles of fifty women editors and reporters, ten of them black.[8]

The best-known woman reporter of the 1880s was Nellie Bly (pen name for Elizabeth Cochrane Seaman, 1865-1922), who travelled around the world in 72 days, 6 hours and 11 minutes, outdoing the dream of Jules Verne's Phineas Fogg. She accomplished this feat between November 1889 and January 1890 as a stunt for Pulitzer's *New York World*. However sensational Nellie Bly's feat was, most women journalists in the 1890s were relegated to women's feature pages, forced to cover society events, and comment on food and fashions. According to newspaperwoman Ishbel Ross:

> By the end of the golden nineties it was either clothes and the cookery book, or the stunt girl . . . there was a sharp division between the sober and the sensational press . . . next to society, the most important funtion of a woman on a conservative paper was to cover teas and clubs.[9]

By 1885, women journalists, still not welcome in the male press clubs, began forming their own professional press organizations. The first such organization was formed at the World's Industrial and Cotton Centennial in New Orleans. This Woman's International Press Association elected Eliza Jane Nicholson (1849-1896), editor of the *Picayune*, as their first president.[10]

World's fairs in the United States historically provided opportunities for women in the press. At the 1876 Philadelphia Centennial Exposition, issues of *Godey's Lady's Book* and Lucy Stone's *Woman's Journal* were exhibited at the Woman's Building. The Women's Centennial Committee sponsored the periodical called *The New Century for Woman*, devoted "to the industrial interest of women," which editor Sarah F. Hallowell defined in terms of education, jobs and fair compensation.[11]

The 1893 Exposition provided varied journalistic opportunities for women reporters and editors. First, it served as a six-month long news source for journalists, attracting prominent female reporters and editors, as well as relatively unknown part-time writers, to Chicago. Second, at the Woman's Building, women's press organizations had offices, journalists served on the governing Board of Lady Managers, and others gave lectures.

Illumination at Night
Photograph by Frances Benjamin Johnston

Third, away from the Fairgrounds at the Art Institute, journalists and editors participated in educational meetings, including a press congress that drew female participants from the United States, Europe, Canada, and Japan.

In addition to the opportunities afforded by the Fair to members of the press, women leaders learned the power of the press, and often developed very effective means of controlling that power. The leaders of prominent women's organizations that gathered at the Fair frequently controlled the news given their constituents through biased reporting in their official press organs. Examples of such reporting may be found in the *Woman's Journal* of the National American Woman Suffrage Association, the journals of the women's clubs and of the Association of Collegiate Alumnae. Women leaders such as Bertha Palmer, who espoused economic equality of working women; suffragist Susan B. Anthony; and Ida B. Wells, who fought for equality for African-Americans, were simultaneously singled out in the press and learned to manipulate the press to further their own causes.

The 1893 Columbian Exposition provided presswomen with an opportunity to expand their reporting to the varied and complex aspects of the Fair. Fair journalists ranged from full-time reporters of the Fair, to photo-journalists who combined reporting with photographs of the attractive buildings, and literary writers and teachers who wrote a few articles about the Fair. Teresa Dean of Chicago's *Inter-Ocean*, Amy Leslie (pen name for Lillie West, 1855-1939), and Kate Field wrote frequent columns for their papers about the Fair. After the Fair Teresa Dean published her Fair columns in the book *White City Chips* and Amy Leslie collected her columns into *Amy Leslie at the Fair*. Frances Benjamin Johnston (1864-1930s), who worked through the Division of Photography of the Smithsonian Institution, published an article titled "The Evolution of a Great Exposition," in *Demorest's Family Magazine* in April, 1892. Using her own photographs of the Fair, Johnston argued that the innovation of the exposition marked the nineteenth century "as the greatest era of progress and civilization the world has yet known" and acknowledged the role of United States and foreign newspapers in supporting the Fair.[12] Johnston also worked with C. D. Arnold, official photographer for the Fair, who complimented her on the article.

By analyzing Marian Shaw's columns about the exposition, one can, in a sense, hold a mirror to the age and ascertain prevalent views on progress of the races, man's relationship to technology, and the emancipation of women. Shaw's articles expose the 19th century belief in the progress of the Caucasian race in America and Europe as contrasted with the primitive foreign (ethnic) races. At the Fair, this distinction of the races was neatly packaged in the separation of the highly symbolic "White City" with its white, Italian neo-classic buildings, and the Midway, with living exhibits from Java, Samoa, Egypt and other exotic countries. In describing the Midway, Shaw comments that "From the Bedouins of the desert and the South Sea Islanders, one can here trace, from living models, the progress of the human race from savagery and barbarism . . . to a condition still many degrees removed from the advanced civilization of the nineteenth century."[13] Shaw, like other visitors to the Fair, experienced the Midway as a kind of living time-line showing the advances of the races, culminating in the artistic and technological exhibits displayed in the buildings of the "White City."

Historian Robert Rydell has written about the Fair, stressing the difference between the White City and the Midway:

> In the late 19th century generally and at the fair particularly, progress was inextricably tied to American racial attitudes towards different peoples of the nation and world . . . Hailed by many as the greatest ethnological display in the history of the world, the Midway provided visitors with apparent ethnological, scientific sanction for the American image of the non-white world as barbaric and childlike. The Plaisance, in short, served as a convenient moral, cultural, and racial yardstick by which to compare and measure America's achievements with those of other peoples.[14]

The disparity between the Utopian "White City" and the earthly Midway

Esquimaux Village — Cracking the Whip

was worthy of newspaper commentary to Marian Shaw, who inadvertently stumbled into this dichotomy by her initial entry to the Fair through the Midway. Unlike earlier visitors who had entered through the prestigious Court of Honor of the "White City," Shaw approached the Fairgrounds near the Esquimaux Village, exclaiming

> We had expected the glorious panorama of the "White City of the Unsalted Sea," with its glittering domes and towers to burst upon our vision like a thing of beauty. After pushing our way through noisy crowds of street vendors, hack-men and rumbling carts, deafened by the roar of the elevated trains about our heads . . . Nothing more attractive than the rear of some of the state buildings met our eyes . . . it would be well for all visitors to this primitive encampment to follow the example of the Cossacks when they attacked the garlic-eating French battallion—stop their nostrils with clay.[15]

Shaw's sense of shock and distaste contrasted markedly with her later impressions of the "White City," when she quoted the Rev. Mr. Stead that "never, until he reaches the New Jerusalem, does he expect to look upon a scene of such bewildering beauty."[16] Once Shaw reached the "White City," she was filled with admiration for the advances of civilization shown in the varied displays in the buildings. Her yardstick for the progress of 19th century civilization was measured by the technological marvels at the Fair, including the 250 foot Ferris Wheel that had been invented for the Fair, the Yerkes telescope, the 4,500 foot movable sidewalk and the Intramural railway. Like other nineteenth century writers, her reactions to these technological advances combined a sense of fear and awe—fear due to the lack of understanding of the working of the inventions and awe at the power. In writing of Machinery Hall, Shaw states that "To the thousands who, like ourselves, have little or no knowledge of the principles underlying all these wonderful works, this building seems like the mysterious abode of mighty but unseen spirits."[17] She seemed most overawed at the exhibit of "caged lightning," which was, in fact, the first large-scale exhibit of the use of electricity. Marian Shaw wrote of science capturing electricity and making it a "servant of servants," yet warns:

> It is true that like a blind and captive Samson, it sometimes rises in its strength and revenges itself upon its captor, but the close of this century will doubtless see it wholly subdued and obedient to every wish of its master.[18]

Shaw's metaphorical use of Samson to represent the power of electricity is indicative of the intrusion of her classical literary style on objective reporting. Her columns are rife with quotes from the Bible and references to poets and authors such as Wordsworth and Charles Dickens, at odds with 20th century standards of reporting. However, this educated background was not unusual for the nineteenth century newspaperwomen who were often well versed in the classics, history and the Bible,[19] as were many of the female newspaper readers. Shaw described some of these educated women who visited the Fair:

> the school-teacher who is doing violence to her conscience by lingering among these beauties when she ought to be upstairs in the educational department studying statistics; bright, radiant college girls, who are intelligently taking in everything, and adding to their already overstocked mental accumulations . . . [20]

As both a college girl and school-teacher, Shaw was impressed by the progress of women shown in the Woman's Building, signaling the emancipation of woman. By continuing the theme of Darwinian progress, she notes the rise of woman out of servitude and the lessons taught in the exhibits of the Woman's Building:

> They form an object lesson in the history of woman's intellectual development, and present an unanswerable argument to those who have been wont to deny her ability to excel in any line of work outside that of light fancy work or household drudgery.[21]

The Woman's Building did offer an object lesson in the history of woman's intellectual development as shown in the woman's organizational room, the educated women on the governing Board of Lady Managers, the library, and daily lectures. Presswomen, like Marian Shaw, participated in the organizational room through exhibits of the National Press League and the Woman's National Press Federation, which, unfortunately were underused due to the busy schedules of the journalists.[22] Several members of the governing Board of Lady Managers in the Woman's Building were presswomen, including Mary Logan of Washington, D.C., who offered the columns of her *Home Magazine* for coverage of women's events at the Fair, citing the circulation of the magazine of nearly 20,000 copies.[23] The New York Women Managers were primary sponsors of a Woman's Library, which contained over 7,000 books contributed by various states. The library also held two folios listing 3,000 names of women from New York who had contributed to the press, and a third volume listing editors and assistant editors.[24] These pioneering folios also included data about the number of women journalists, the kind of publications which employed them, and the class of positions they held.[25]

Near the Library was an assembly room, in which noontime lectures were presented. Mary Temple Bayard, "Meg" of the *Philadelphia Times,* spoke on "Woman in Journalism," stressing the lack of difference in the qualifications and abilities of men and women reporters, and Madame Fanny Zampini Salazar, publisher of Italy's newspaper *The Queen,* lectured on "Women in Modern Italy." Other speakers included Catherine Cole, who wrote daily letters from the Fair to the New Orleans *Picayune,* and Kate Field (1838-1896), editor of *Kate Field's Washington,* who spoke of her own efforts to publicize the Fair, and encouraged audience members to advertise the Fair.[26] The effectiveness of these lectures is difficult to ascertain since they neither attracted press coverage, nor were they organized around central topics.

The largest venue for the presentation of women journalists was at the six-month women's congresses or educational meetings, held at the Art Institute. The motto of the congresses was "Not matter, but mind," and they addressed the mental and educational status of the nations in contrast to the buildings of the "White City" like the Woman's Building, which presented material exhibits of arts, handicrafts, and technology. Thirty educational meetings were held on topics of interest to women ranging from suffrage and temperance to the arts and the press. The first congress was "The Congress of Representative Women" held from May 15 to May 21, which was run by committees from the National Council of Women (NCW), which was comprised primarily of suffragists, and the General Federation of Women's Clubs (GFWC).

The opening of the women's congresses was covered by the major national newspapers, with *The New York Times* reporting that "This congress will be in earnest and the women who are here have come to Chicago with the idea of doing all in their power to advance the interests of the women of the world."[27] At this meeting, Emmeline Wells spoke on "Western Women Authors and Journalists," chronicling the beginning of the Utah *Woman's*

Kate Field

Exponent in 1872, and her editorship of that newspaper. Belle Armstrong gave a history of the New England Woman's Press Association, and John Strange Winter (Henrietta E. V. Stannard) of England told of the difficulties of starting the Writer's Club, a woman's press club in London.[28]

At the close of the Congress of Representative Women, there was a press congress held from May 23 to May 27, which included daily press, weeklies, magazines, religious press, and trade, scientific and professional journals. Women met alone in the morning and joined with men during the evening sessions. The women's congresses were held under the auspices of the Woman's Branch of the World's Congress Auxiliary, directed by Ellen Henrotin, who stated:

> In no calling have women attained more distinction than as journalists; a profession for which they are admirably adapted. It is astonishing how great a number of women are constantly entering the profession; and this international meeting can only result in great good to themselves, as it will emphasize their strength.[29]

During the congress of "Press Women of the World," Antoinette Wakeman of *The Evening Post*, Mary Krout of the Chicago *Inter-Ocean*, Olive Logan from London, and journalists from Stockholm, France, Canada and Japan all spoke. Teresa Dean, in her column "White City Chips" of the *Inter-Ocean*, reported on the success of Canadian Eva Brodlique's paper and especially on Mrs. Swalm's essay on "The Newspaper as a Factor of Civilization." She commented, however, that "Men were rather scarce articles among the audience, but those who were there and those who tiptoed up to look in at the door behaved very well and appeared to be much interested."[30]

The evening of May 23rd, at a general press congress of men and women, a paper by Mrs. E. J. Nicholson (1849-1896), editor of the New Orleans *Picayune*, was read by Catherine Cole. The topic was "Woman as a Newspaper Proprietor and Editor." Nicholson represented the administrative side of women's journalism, as the first woman publisher of an important U.S. daily—a role she inherited after her husband died. She founded the Women's International Press Association in 1887, as an outgrowth of the Women's National Press Association which began at the World's Fair in New Orleans in 1885.[31] Not only did Nicholson have a paper read at the 1893 press congress, but she had a newspaper exhibit at the Fair.

On May 24th Jennie June Croly spoke at the women's press congress on "Editorial and Department Work," and at a department congress Sally Joy White lectured on "The Woman's Page." One essay that excited great interest was Kate Field's address of May 25th on "A Woman's paper versus a Paper for Women." Kate Field, in residence at the Lexington Hotel from May to November, had made herself a factor in the progress of the Fair. Even before the Fair began, women officials at the Fair relied on her support through her paper. In March, 1892 Bertha Palmer thanked her for her clipping from *Kate Field's Washington* and her journalistic efforts to support women at the Fair.[32]

The Union Signal, the W.C.T.U. organ, reported on Kate Field's address, stressing Field's support of suffrage limited by educational tests, not universal suffrage. The *Signal* went on to report that after the Republican convention in Louisville, Field was ready to join Anthony, who was in the audience: "Then verily the floor seemed to rise and the roof to come down and no sign of order appeared until Miss Anthony stood upon the platform and took Miss Field's hand."[33] This public support of suffrage by a prominent newspaper woman was an important news item, since Field had initially appeared to support the Board of Lady Managers (who repeatedly avoided supporting suffrage in the Woman's Building, even denying the NAWSA space for an exhibit).

At the same time these newspapers, magazines, and journals reported news of interest to women from the Fair, female leaders at the Fair were savvy to the power of the press, and attempted to use the press to advance their own causes. Several major women's organizations held their national meetings at the Fair, and reported on the success of their particular meetings and causes to their members, often ignoring those of competing organizations. The journals of both the NAWSA and the GFWC reported extensively on their annual meetings and the importance of their own leaders at the Exposition. The pro-suffrage *Woman's Journal* and the *Woman's Tribune* published accounts of the Congress of Representative Women, at which Susan B. Anthony spoke. Pro-suffrage biases can be noted in the way in which two prominent women journalists handled their reports of Anthony's impact at the congresses. London correspondent Florence Fenwick Miller singled out Anthony as the veteran leader of American women suffragists.[34] *Inter-Ocean* editor Mary Krout glorified Anthony's contributions at the Fair:

> When it is asked what woman was the most prominent, most honored, most in demand in all the public ceremonials and private functions held in Chicago during the Columbian Exposition, there can be but one answer — Susan B. Anthony.[35]

Conversely, *The New Cycle*, the organ for the General Federation of Women's Clubs (GFWC), reflecting its avoidance of a pro-suffrage stance in 1893, did not mention suffrage. Instead it detailed the minutes of the annual meeting of the GFWC at the Fair at which editor Jennie June Croly lobbied for finances and support for its paper, *The New Cycle*, as an organ of the women's federated club system.

> There is to-day but one recognized channel of public discourse—the press. Our two hundred clubs scattered over the breadth of the country can be brought to concerted action in anything, only through some general medium of communication. For our clubs, as clubs, there exists but one available organ—the *New Cycle*.[36]

Both the women's suffrage movement and club movement understood the influence of the press as a means of communication to their constituents and

Susan B. Anthony
Photograph by Frances Benjamin Johnston

influence of the press as a means of communication to their constituents and as a rallying point to their cause.

At the same time that women leaders were featured news in the women's press organs and general newspapers worldwide, these same reformers and civic leaders learned the importance of the support of the press, and ways to manipulate that support. Bertha Palmer, president of the Board of Lady Managers in the Woman's Building, was concerned about the loyalty of her press committee. In choosing a press bureau, Palmer wanted to avoid duplicating membership with the press bureau of the rival Queen Isabella Association, which had lobbied unsuccessfully with Susan B. Anthony and other suffragists to represent women at the Fair. During the Fair there was a continuing rivalry with the Isabellas, who were the business and professional women and suffragists. At their own club house off the Fairgrounds the Isabellas appointed a press bureau which included suffragist Sally Joy White of the *Boston Post* and Catherine Cole of the New Orleans *Picayune*.

Palmer and other members of the Board of Lady Managers wanted journalists who would be loyal to them and their interests. As she wrote to her vice-president, Ellen Henrotin:

> I enclose you an article . . . which appeared in the Inter Ocean of Feb. 14th written by Mrs. Krout about the press Association of the Isabellas—marked "Exhibit B," in which you will notice that they have most of the names we were considering for our Press Committee. I think it most important that our Press Committee be loyal to a degree and I don't know that I would quite feel that we could trust anyone that is or has been a member of the Isabela [sic] Association to represent our cause in its strongest light before the public . . . We must make no mistake about this matter as it will not do to have our own numbers writing us down instead of up.[37]

Palmer's fears proved to be well founded. After Mrs. Palmer and members of her Board attempted to consolidate power in an executive committee, they met opposition from the Board's secretary, Phoebe Couzins, a lawyer and suffragist. In April, 1891, Couzins was fired for her opposition and promptly filed a lawsuit against Palmer and her Board, receiving the support of the Isabellas. The *Queen Isabella Journal*, as well as other national papers, published articles supporting Couzins, including a pro-Couzins resolution by the professional and business women of the Isabella Association.

Palmer learned the importance of garnering a press loyal to her interests through this experience. She even proposed a national press bureau for the Woman's Building to Mary Krout, one of the Board's lady managers and editor of the "Woman's Kingdom" department of the Chicago *Inter-Ocean*:

> The Board of Lady Managers is favorably considering creating an organized press bureau in each state by bringing together the women writers who may be appointed to represent them by each of the strong papers. If these state branches could be welded into one whole, it would make a strong organization of press women, whose influence and power would be almost irresistable. Hoping that

all the press women of the country may unite with the Board of Lady Managers in what they are trying to accomplish . . . [38]

The reciprocity of gain to both sides is most evident in this letter. While Palmer did attract negative press comments for her handling of Phoebe Couzins, she later became the darling of Chicago press, dubbed "Chicago's queen." At the opening ceremonies on May 1st her speech dedicating the Woman's Building was printed in full, as were extensive descriptions of her sumptuous gowns and jewels at all public appearances she made at the women's congresses.

Susan B. Anthony was an important subject of the news throughout her four month stay at the Fair. On one occasion, she tapped press coverage to present a radical new direction for journalism. On May 23rd, at the end of the morning women's press congress, chairman Mary Krout mentioned that Anthony was present and asked her to speak. One newspaper reported on Anthony's impromptu speech:

> Miss Anthony's central idea . . . was her proposition to establish a daily newspaper in Chicago which would be owned, edited and run by women. It would not be a woman suffrage paper—Miss Anthony is too old in her work to try to work over an old idea—but a newspaper. The business manager was to be a woman; the clerical force to be women; the managing editor a woman; the editorial corps, women; the city editor, a woman; the reporters, women. It would be a newspaper in which every item should be written from a woman's point of view . . . Perhaps there would be newsgirls to sell this paper.[39]

The Fair had sparked Anthony's confidence in the ability of Chicago to generate such a paper, due to Chicago's success in mounting the world's Fair. She was later quoted by the *Chicago Daily Tribune* on May 28th, on the differences in attitude between women and men towards the news: "I wouldn't have a whole page blistered over with murders and criminal assaults and thefts." When asked if the paper would advocate woman suffrage, she answered "It would advocate absolute equality of all human beings . . . the legislation of our country is all wrong. That is to say, it is made for one class. You legislate for a class—for men."[40]

Two aspects of Anthony's proposal address unique issues. First, she suggested an all-female paper that was not an arm of a specific cause, suggesting an equality beyond reform issues. Second, Anthony's proposal reveals a fundamental difference in her perception of news interests of men and women. She emphasized men's reporting of violence as news. Although Anthony's newspaper concept was not realized in Chicago, her proposal reflects a Utopian atmosphere fueled by the Columbian Exposition.

Bertha Palmer and Susan B. Anthony received prominent coverage in the women's journals and national newspapers due to their official positions at the fair. However, no African-American women, except one lady manager from New York, had an official position at the exposition. When several

African-American women's organizations requested representation at the Woman's Building, their requests were denied. At the Congress of Representative Women, Frances Harper spoke, and Ida Tims Klocker gave an essay on "Woman as a Race Reporter" at the woman's press congress. Nonetheless, the most prominent African-American woman leader was excluded from all the congresses and from the Woman's Building. That woman was journalist and editor Ida B. Wells, who had railed in the press against the lynchings of Afro-American men.

Denied an official voice at the 1893 Exposition, Wells joined with Frederick Douglass, and her fiancé, Chicago lawyer Ferdinand Barnett, to publish the pamphlet *The Reason Why the Colored American is Not in the World's Columbian*

Ida B. Wells

Exposition. Wells passed out nearly 10,000 pamphlets to visitors at the Haitian building where Frederick Douglass gave her a desk (Douglass had been the American minister to Haiti from 1889-1891). They used this pamphlet, and the subsequent press it drew, as a formal protest against the exclusion of Afro-Americans at the Fair. Douglass and Wells tried to solicit support and financial contributions from the Negro press for the pamphlet. Editors from the *Methodist Union* and *Indianapolis Freeman* condemned the suggestion, but several newspapers, including the *Cleveland Gazette* and the *Philadelphia Tribune*, did encourage support of the pamphlet.[41]

Wells wrote the preface to explain the reason for the pamphlet, asking the question

> Why are not the colored people, who constitute so large an element of the American population, and who have contributed so large a share to American greatness,—more visibly present and better represented in this World's Exposition?[42]

Wells' main contribution to the pamphlet was a chapter on "Lynch Law," complete with statistics on lynching and the crimes with which the victims were charged, and a graphic photograph of a lynching. This pamphlet was intended for visitors from England, France, and Spain, to whom Wells wanted to appeal for financial support. Serving as a rallying press organ, *The Reason Why* heralded the injustices against her people before Wells' trip to London later in the summer to solicit foreign support.

Ida Wells also resented the treatment of Afro-Americans at the Fair, and especially the condescending Colored Jubilee Day planned for August, 1893. She accused Fair officials of using two thousand watermelons to bring lower-class Afro-Americans to the celebration. *The Cleveland Gazette* and *Topeka Call* reported her outrage:

> The self-respect of the race is sold for a mess of pottage and the spectacle of the class of our people who will come on that excursion roaming around the grounds munching watermelon will do more to lower the race in the estimation of the world than anything else . . . [giving] our enemies all the illustration they wish as excuse for not treating the Afro-American with the equality of other citizens.[43]

Denied an official voice, Ida B. Wells fought for the rights of her people through her pamphlet and through the public press.

For women at the 1893 World's Columbian Exposition, newspapers, magazines, pamphlets, and organizational journals became tools to further their careers and causes. The six-month Fair, which was covered by papers nationwide, drew leading female journalists and editors like Kate Field, Jennie June Croly, Amy Leslie, and Teresa Dean who reported the on-going events of the Fair. The woman's press had official status in the Woman's Building through a press bureau, in organizational exhibits, and with featured speakers at the lecture series. The inclusion of women journalists in various congresses, and the scheduling of a special women's press congress attest to the importance afforded women journalists at the Fair, and in the 1890s. One female journalist wrote of the effect of the Fair on newspaper-women:

> That the Columbian Exposition will be the means of adding to the numbers and influence of newspaper women . . . and in uniting them in closer bonds of fellowship and stimulating their loyalty to high ideals for the sake of their chosen profession and their beloved land, is a foregone conclusion.[44]

While newspaper women were reporting on the Fair in general and receiving official status at this major international event, their columns reflect a strong interest in women leaders and women's activities at the exposition. Bertha Palmer, Susan B. Anthony, and Ida B. Wells were savvy to the power of the press, and their causes received repeated coverage in general newspapers as well as in women's journals. Presswomen, women leaders and readers alike understood that for those who could not come to the Fair, or who could not stay for the entire six months, the newspapers and magazines were their window on the Fair.

NOTES

Ann E. Feldman is a cultural historian, and currently Visiting Scholar at the Chicago Humanities Institute, University of Chicago. For the past seven years she has researched and produced several projects about women leaders at the 1893 World's Fair, including a musical theater show "Politics and Old Lace" which premiered at University of Chicago in April, 1992 and a recording of women's chamber music from the Fair, entitled "Women at an Exposition." Dr. Feldman has also lectured extensively on various aspects of women's leadership at the Fair, published an article for Music Library Associations *Notes*, and is presently writing a book *The Power of Associations: World's Fair Women in 1893*, assisted by Julia Kramer. The author is grateful to the following individuals for their assistance: Julia Kramer, Visiting Scholar, Chicago Humanities Institute, University of Chicago; Eileen Ogintz, freelance reporter; and Dr. Carolyn DeSwarte Gifford, editor for the Frances Willard *Journals*.

1. Handy, Major Moses P. *First Decennium of National Editorial Association of the United States*, (Chicago, 1896), Vol. 1, 477. Chicago Historical Society.

2. Dean, Teresa. *White City Chips*, (Chicago, Warren Publishing Co., 1895), 408-411.

3. Beasley, Maurine and Silver, Sheila. *Women in Media: A Documentary Source Book*. (Washington, D.C.: Women's Institute for Freedom of the Press, 1979), 38.

4. Marzolf, Marion. "The Woman Journalist: Colonial Printer to City Desk," *Journalism History*, Vol. 1, No. 3 (Autumn 1974), 102.

5. Smith, Henry Ladd. "The Beauteous Jennie June: Pioneer Woman Journalist," *Journalism Quarterly*, 40 (Spring 1963), 172.

6. Ross, Ishbel. *Ladies of the Press*, (New York and London: Harper & Bros., Publishers, 1936), 45.

7. Tucker, David M. "Miss Ida B. Wells and Memphis Lynching," *Phylon* XXXII, No. 2 (Summer 1971), 113.

8. Marzolf, 103.

9. Ross, 17-19.

10. Bridges, Lamar W. "Eliza Jane Nicholson of the 'Picayune,'" *Journalism History*, Vol. 2, No. 4 (Winter 1975-1976), 115.

11. Post, Robert C. ed. *1876 - A Centennial Exposition*. Washington, D.C.: Smithsonian Institution (1976), 171.

12. Frances Benjamin Johnston. "The Evolution of a Great Exposition," *Demorest's Family Magazine*, Vol. XXVIII, No. 6 (April 1892), 319-320 in Frances Benjamin Johnston Papers, Microfilm 33:6, Collections of the Manuscript Division, Library of Congress, Washington, D. C.

13. Shaw, Marian, *World's Fair Notes*, 56.

14. Rydell, Robert W. "The World's Columbian Exposition of 1893: Racist Underpinnings of a Utopian Artifact," 3-4, in Alice Fletcher Papers, National Museum of American History Archives, Smithsonian Institution, Washington, D. C.; *Journal of American Culture*, Vol. 1 (1978), 255.

15. Shaw, 15.

16. Shaw, 23.

17. Shaw, 32.

18. Shaw, 45.

19. Belford, Barbara. *Brilliant Bylines, A Biographical Anthology of Notable Newspaperwomen in America*, (New York: Columbia University Press, 1986), xii.

20. Shaw, 38.

21. Shaw, 61.

22. Elliott, Maud Howe, ed. *Art and Handicraft in the Woman's Building*, (Paris & New York: Goupil & Co., Boussod, Valadon & Co., Successors, 1893), 156.

23. Notes from meeting, September 10, 1891. Board of Lady Managers, World's Columbian Exposition, Vol. 6, 5-6. Chicago Historical Society.

24. *Ibid*, 118.

25. Wing, Amelia K. "The Work of the Women's Board of Managers for the World's Fair," *The New Cycle*, Vol. 6, No. 3 (April 1893), 353-354.

26. Field, Miss Kate. "A Talk," in *The Congress of Women held in the Woman's Building*, Mary K.O. Eagle, ed. (Washington, D.C.: W. B. Conkey, 1894), 78-79.

27. Susan B. Anthony. Remarks on World's Columbian Exposition, World's Congress of Representative Women, *The New York Times*, May 13, 1893, in *The Papers of Elizabeth Cady Stanton and Susan B. Anthony*, Also in Microfilm Series 3, 31: 446.27. Patricia B. Holland and Ann D. Gordon, eds. (Wilmington, Del.: Scholarly Resources, Inc., 1989).

28. Sewall, May Wright, ed. *The World's Congress of Representative Women*, (Chicago and New York: Rand, McNally & Co., 1894), II: 800-802, 806-815.

29. "Dear Madame," from Woman's Branch of World's Congress Auxiliary by Mrs. Henrotin, World's Columbian Exposition, December 19, 1892 - December 31, 1892, Palmer Collection, Folders 3, 4. Chicago Historical Society.

30. Dean, 85.

31. Marzolf, 101-102.

32. Whiting, Lilian. *Kate Field*, (Boston: Little, Brown & Co., 1899), 497.

33. World's Columbian Exposition, Public and Religious Press Congresses. B. V. Cushman, "Columbian Crumbs," *Union Signal* (Chicago), June 15, 1893, in Susan B. Anthony Papers, Microfilm, Series 3, 31: 483.

34. Harper, Ida Husted. *Life and Work of Susan B. Anthony*, (Indianapolis: Bowen-Merrill, 1899), II: 747-748.

35. Harper, 752.

36. "Minutes of the Congress of General Federation of Woman's Clubs, held in Chicago, May 18, 1893," *The New Cycle*, Vol. VI, No. 4 (May 1893), 465.

37. Bertha Palmer to Mrs. Henrotin, World's Columbian Exposition, Board of Lady Managers, Box 3, Vol. 9 (December 3, 1890 - February 21, 1891), 434-436. Chicago Historical Society.

38. Bertha Palmer to Miss Krout, October 27, 1891. World's Columbian Exposition, Board of Lady Managers, Box 3, Vol. 109, 921-922. Chicago Historical Society.

39. World's Columbian Exposition, Public Press Congress, *Chicago Daily Tribune*, May 23, 1893 (?) in Susan B. Anthony Papers, Microfilm. Series 3, 31: 477-478.

40. "Interview on Ideal Newspaper," *Chicago Daily Tribune*, May 28, 1893, in Susan B. Anthony Papers, Microfilm, Series 3, 31: 485. A contemporary reference to a similar issue arises in Nan Robertson, *The Girls in the Balcony* (New York: Random House, 1992), 144. Robertson writes that the inequities of a male-controlled newspa-

per system were still being questioned in 1972, when *The New York Times* was sued for sex discrimination by its women journalists, with reporter Betsy Wade complaining that the problem was a newspaper that spoke with a "white male voice."

41. Rudwick, Elliott M. and August Meier. "Black Man in the 'White City,' Negroes and the Columbian Exposition, 1893," *Phylon*, 26, No.4 (1965), 356.

42. Wells, Ida B. and Frederick Douglass. *The Reason Why the Colored American is Not in the World's Columbian Exposition*, (Chicago: Privately Printed, 1893), 1.

43. *Cleveland Gazette*, July 15, 22, 1893 and *Topeka Call*, July 15, 1893, cited in Rudwick, 360.

44. Dickinson, Susan E. "Women Journalists in America," in *The National Exposition Souvenir, What America Owes to Women*, Lydia Hoyt Farmer, ed. (Buffalo: Charles Wells Moulton, 1893), 211.

BIBLIOGRAPHY

(a) The Search for Marian Shaw:

Archives, Minnesota Historical Society. World's Columbian Exposition, 1893, box 2, literature.

Archives, Minnesota Historical Society. Records of the Minnesota World's Fair Board and the Minnesota Board of Lady Managers, Guest Registers, Volumes B and C.

Bancroft, Hubert Howe. *The Book of the Fair*, 1893. New York: Bounty Books (Reprint) p. 44, 133, 287.

Boston Evening Transcript, December 20, 1884, p. 10; December 27, 1884, p. 4; and January 15, 1885, p. 4.

Campbell, J. B. *Campbell's Illustrated History of the World's Columbian Exposition*. 2 Vols. Philadelphia: Sessler & Dongan, 1894.

Dickinson, Susan E. "Women Journalists in America," in Farmer, pp. 205-211.

Farmer, Lydia Hoyt, ed. *The National Exposition Souvenir: What America Owes to Women*. New York: Charles Wells Moulton, 1893, pp. 208-209.

Fargo Daily Argus, June 7, 1894 (The "Fire Edition".)

Hill, James J., Papers. James J. Hill Reference Library, St. Paul, Minnesota. [Files relating to *The Argus* of Fargo, North Dakota.]

Minneapolis Central High School Yearbook, 1892, p. 54.

Minneapolis Journal, June 9, 1900; April 19 and 20, 1901.

Minneapolis Tribune, April 19, 20, and 21, 1901.

Minnesota Daily, April 23, 1901.

Moline, Melva. *The Forum, First Hundred Years*. Fargo: privately printed, 1979.

The New York Times, April 19, 1885.

Scott County (Minnesota) *Argus*, July 6, 1893.

Shaw, Marian. *Queen Bess, Or, What's In A Name*. New York: G. P. Putnam's Sons, 1885.

Shaw, Marian. *Latin Prose Composition For Cicero Classes*. Minneapolis: Board of Education, 1899.

Weimann, Jeanne Madeline. *The Fair Women*. Chicago: Academy Chicago, 1981.

White, Trumbull and Igleheart, William. *The World's Columbian Exposition, Chicago, 1893*. Philadelphia: J. H. Moore & Co., 1893. p. 617.

_____ *History of the Minnesota Horticultural Society*. St. Paul: St. Paul Press Company, 1873, pp. 186-188.

_____ *Handbook to the World's Columbian Exposition*. Chicago: Rand McNally & Co., 1893.

_____ *List of Books Sent by Home and Foreign Committees to the Library of the Woman's Building*. Chicago: World's Columbian Exposition, 1893, p. 12, 18.

_____ *Official Catalogue of the Illinois Woman's Exposition Board*. Chicago: W. B. Conkey Company, 1893, p. 25.

_____ *Catalogue of the Wisconsin State Normal School at Platteville, Grant County, Wis. For the Academic Years 1866-7 and 1867-8*. Platteville, Wis.: M. P. Rindlaub, Witness Office, 1868.

(b) Women and the Press at the 1893 World's Columbian Exposition:

Beasley, Maurine and Silver, Sheila. *Women in Media: A Documentary Source Book*. Washington, D.C.: Women's Institute for Freedom of the Press, 1979.

Belford, Barbara. *Brilliant Bylines, A Biographical Anthology of Notable Newspaperwomen in America*. New York: Columbia University Press, 1986.

Bennion, Sherilyn Cox. *Equal to the Occasion: Women Editors of the Nineteenth Century West*. Reno and Las Vegas: University of Nevada Press, 1990.

Bennion, Sherilyn Cox. "A Working List of Women Editors of the 19th Century West," *Journalism History*, Vol. 7, No. 2 (Summer 1980), 60-65.

Bridges, Lamar W. "Eliza Jane Nicolson of the 'Picayune,'" *Journalism History*, 2, No. 4 (Winter 1975-76), 110-115.

Chicago. World's Columbian Exposition, 1893, World's Congress Auxiliary, Department of the Public Press. *Program of Public Press Congress*, 11-19. Chicago Historical Society.

Dean, Teresa. *White City Chips*, Chicago: Warren Publishing Co., 1895.

Dean, Teresa, papers. Archives, Northwestern University Library Special Collections.

Dickinson, Susan E. "Women Journalists in America," in *The National Exposition Souvenir, What America Owes to Women*, Lydia Hoyt Farmer, ed. Buffalo: Charles Wells Moulton, 1893, 206–211.

Duster, Alfreda M., ed. *Crusade for Justice: The Autobiography of Ida B. Wells*. Chicago: University of Chicago Press, 1970.

Elliott, Maud Howe, ed. *Art and Handicraft in the Woman's Building*. Paris & New York: Goupil & Co., Boussod, Valadon & Co., Successors, 1893.

Handy, Major Moses P., Chief of the Bureau of Publicity and Promotion. *First Decennium of National Editorial Association of the United States*. Vol. 1, 1896. Chicago Historical Society.

Harper, Ida Husted. *Life and Work of Susan B. Anthony*, Vol. 2. Salem, New Hampshire: Ayer Co., Publishers, Inc. Reprint Edition, 1983.

Holland, Patricia B. and Ann D. Gordon, eds. *The Papers of Elizabeth Cady Stanton and Susan B. Anthony*. Wilmington, Del.: Scholarly Resources Inc., 1989. Microfilm. Series 1, 3.

Humphreys, Nancy K. *American Women's Magazines, An Annotated Historical Guide*. New York and London: Garland Publishing, Inc. 1989.

Jordan, Elizabeth G. "The Newspaper Woman's Story" [Journalist Series], *Lippincott's Monthly Magazine*, II (January-June 1893), 340-347.

The Journalist, Vol. 8, No. 19, January 26, 1889. "Woman's Number."

Marzolf, Marion. *Up From the Footnote: A History of Women Journalists*. New York: Hastings House, Publishers, 1977.

Marzolf, Marion. "The Woman Journalist: Colonial Printer to City Desk," *Journalism History*, Vol. 1, No. 3 (Autumn 1974), 100-107.

Marzolf, Marion, comp. "The Literature of Women in Journalism History: A Supplement," *Journalism History*, Vol. 3, No. 4 (Winter 1976-77), 116-120.

Marzolf, Marion, Ramona R. Rush and Darlene Stern, comps. "The Literature of Women in Journalism History," *Journalism History*, Vol. 1, No. 4 (Winter 1974-75), 117-128.

Masel-Walters, Lynne. "A Burning Cloud by Day: The History and Content of the 'Woman's Journal'," *Journalism History*, Vol. 3, No. 4 (Winter 1976), 103-110.

Mather, Anne. "A History of Feminist Periodicals, Part 1," *Journalism History*, Vol. 1, No. 3 (Autumn 1974), 82-85.

New Cycle, Vol. IV, No. 4 (May 1893), Washington, D.C.: Archives, General Federation of Women's Clubs.

Palmer, Bertha Honore Collection. Chicago, World's Columbian Exposition of 1893, Board of Lady Managers, Chicago Historical Society.

Penn, L. Garland. *The Afro-American Press, and Its Editors*. Springfield, Massachusetts: Willey & Co., Publishers, 1891.

Pride, Armistead S., comp. "The Black Press to 1968: A Bibliography," *Journalism History*, Vol. 4, No. 4 (Winter 1977-78) 148-155.

Robertson, Nan. *The Girls in the Balcony*. New York: Random House, 1992.

Ross, Ishbel. *Ladies of the Press*. New York and London: Harper & Bros, Publishers, 1936.

Schilpp, Madelon Golden and Sharon M. Murphy. *Great Women of The Press*. Carbondale and Edwardsville: Southern Illinois University Press, 1983.

Smith, Henry Ladd. "The Beauteous Jennie June: Pioneer Woman Journalist," *Journalism Quarterly* 40 (Spring 1963), 169-174.

Wells, Ida B. and Frederick Douglass. *The Reason Why the Colored American is not in the World's Columbian Exposition*. Chicago: privately printed, 1893.

Whiting, Lilian. *Kate Field*. Boston: Little, Brown & Co., 1899.

Willard, Frances. "Rationale of Woman's Opportunity in Journalism," *Independent* (New York), September 16, 1886, 4-5.

Zuckerman, Mary Ellen, comp. *Sources on the History of Women's Magazines, 1792-1960, An Annotated Bibliography*. New York, Westport, & London: Greenwood Press, 1991.

Index